PARENT'S GUIDE: INNER ANCHOR

TIPS FOR IDENTIFYING AND OVERCOMING A DAUGHTER'S BULIMIA NERVOSA

SHANNON MICHELLE

INTRODUCTION

There are few things more terrifying in life than the realization that your child is at the mercy of an eating disorder. It's something no parent is prepared for and there's little that can be said to ease the immense pressure we feel as the responsible adult in a situation like this. Being seemingly powerless in such a time sensitive situation is immensely draining and can take a serious strain on your mental health. It's key to remember you're human too and you're hurting as well as your child. Playing the blame game with yourself is not going to help you or your daughter. However, all hope is not lost. Knowledge and empathy are your greatest weapons when fighting against this disorder, the keys to both follow in the chapters ahead. There are practical steps you can take to regain some footing in this situation and in turn guide and support your child through the tender and chaotic realities of living with Bulimia Nervosa.

WHAT IS BULIMIA NERVOSA?

*B*ulimia Nervosa is a mental health condition characterized by an inaccurate negative self-image and disordered habits surrounding food. The sufferer of Bulimia Nervosa has body dysmorphia; this is an inability, rather than a choice, to see your true self. Many parents sadly rule this out as being teenage stubbornness. They try to help their teen by telling them they don't need to change and when their daughter can't agree with them, they simplify her actions to her being a teenager. This is incredibly harmful, as your daughter is not the one guiding this thought pattern or belief. The mind itself inflates the perceived imperfections and flaws to make them feel overwhelmingly large. Someone struggling with a dysmorphic self-image may spend long periods of time looking in mirrors or getting dressed, as they hyper focus on their insecurities. Another common way that this is shown is through projection. If your child frequently comments on other's appearances, this may be people in the street or on tv, this is another telling sign that they are feeling insecure in their own physical appearance and are projecting those insecurities onto others. They're not meaning to be overly critical or hurtful to anybody else, they're just noticing the perceived flaws that they see in themselves, in others.

Disordered eating is easily brushed off as small things that are "one offs" but if you pay closer attention, a pattern emerges. Fixed routines surrounding meal times, portion sizes, counting calories, 'playing' with food on the plate, avoiding or restricting carbohydrates or fats and sugars, frequent weighing, binge eating and purging are all associated with having an eating disorder. For me personally, my eating issues began at age eleven, in middle school and would continue for the following two years. My disordered eating first made an appearance in the form of cutting down or removing some of my main meals, breakfast was limited to the bare minimum and lunch was often non-existent. When I got home from school I'd snack up until dinner was ready and then eat my dinner with my family. To them it probably looked as though I was eating if anything, more than normal. Little did they know I was starving myself for much of my day and purging after mealtimes. My stereo would accompany me to the bathroom after meals, paired with a running shower I was able to drown out the morbid sounds of me retching and keep my family off the main scent. I would also weigh myself beforehand, hoping for the numbers to have dropped every day. From an exterior view, I was a teenage girl taking a shower with her music on and who appeared to be eating well. My Bulimia was elusive to my parents who only recognized a change in me when my disorder had shaved pounds off me and my frame was barely recognizable.

One of the largest hurdles to overcome in getting your daughter help is the recognition stage. First, realizing what she is doing and then recognizing that for what it is, is a severely underrated step. It's common for parents to teeter on the edge of uncertainty for a long time. Taking that plunge into the unknown world of eating disorders and Bulimia is a seriously brave step for a parent to make but ultimately the right one. You know your daughter best and if you've seen a change in her behavior that leads you to seriously question if she has an eating disorder, you're most probably right. Taking some time to think it through isn't a bad thing though, just make sure that if you do have concerns that you act on them in some way sooner rather than later. It is important to take that time to think it through logically, as sometimes our love for our children can blur reality and make it easy to invent problems from small inconsistencies. We love them and care for them deeply, it's a natural part of having children, sometimes we snowball things that don't need to be compiled. Don't avoid your feelings and suspicions though if you're still feeling sure that something more is afoot with your daughter's mental and physical health.

Many eating disorders in general fixate and thrive on numbers, repetitions and patterns; this differs slightly with bulimia nervosa, although purging and binging habits are often well established within a routine or schedule. With bulimia nervosa the feeling of being "out of control" is sky high, as the sufferer binges and purges they are left in a continual cycle of feeling out of control with their eating and trying to "make up" for that behavior with more purging. The purging however is soon followed by hunger and the need to eat or binge again; shame follows soon after. Alone, this cruel cycle is nearly impossible to break away from. My meals soon would turn into a repeating pattern of having nothing but a slim fast shake for both breakfast and lunch, the only solid food I was eating was with my family at dinner time or the snacks I gorged on when I binged beforehand. All of which would be purged away anyway, and my consistent weighing aided in all of my habits rapidly becoming a fixation. This cycle would continue throughout high school. The pattern of feeling overly full after dinner would be the trigger for my habits, this feeling was what made breaking the mold so difficult. The unbearable shame and physical discomfort that came from this feeling was what I would spend the next seven years habitually attempting to outrun and avoid. That and the hatred I felt for the bloated body that stood opposite me in the mirror. I would spend time everyday pinpointing parts of my body that my mind deemed "too fat" and would try everything I could to change that. Heartburn, a desperate hunger and headaches plagued me relentlessly throughout the height of my disorder but the positive comments from my peers only fueled the fire in my Bulimic mind. I lived for external validation while my interior happiness was fading further and further away from reach. It is a scary thought to ponder about where I could have ended up had I not managed to change my self-destructive habits, this is exactly why giving your daughters medical and emotional support is so crucial. So that those agonizing thoughts of how she could possibly end up, don't become a heartbreaking reality.

Humans are creatures of comfort and routine; our habits create a safe 'controlled' space for us and deviating from them (especially with desperately poor self-esteem at risk) is a mammoth task. It's not as simple as being told that what you're doing is bad for you and then making a change, if the world were that simple then no one would drink, smoke or gamble. It takes serious work to regain a healthier mindset with food, it's something that can take years to make progress with and some never fully shake their problematic tendencies with food. Acknowledgment and education can be life changing for sufferers though, self-awareness and being aware of possible environmental triggers will go a long way towards a better relationship with food.

Bulimia Nervosa comes with a vicious internal self-dialogue. When you attempt to miss a purge or binge session your inner voice comes out to gaslight, manipulate, mock and shame you into following suit with the disordered activities. Parents should be sure not to confuse this as a child's stubbornness or unwillingness to change, there will be a terrifying fear of deviating from what the eating disorder is telling you to do. When you're in the midst of the disorder, it feels incredibly uncomfortable and intimidating to stray away from what this voice is grooming you into believing. Teens can easily feel isolated and withdraw when the draining presence of the eating disorder is met with misunderstandings from family members. I would always order salads when out to dinner with my family, as they stopped me from experiencing the heavy feeling I resented so much, but ridicule from my family paired with my already self-destructive mind meant my happiness slipped further from view. The bulimic voice is incredibly good at what it does, it is nowhere near as easy to just ignore it. Be open minded, empathetic and understanding. Although they have an eating disorder, they're still a person and beneath that a hurting child.

Intervention, medical attention, counseling, therapy and support from family and friends give the person struggling with Bulimia the strongest chance of regulating and overcoming their issues surrounding food and self.

What are the recognized symptoms of Bulimia Nervosa?

- Binge eating.
- Purging.
- Excessive exercise.
- Abusing laxatives.
- Scared of putting on weight.
- Being critical and self-conscious of yourself and others.
- Mood swings.
- Obsessing about food and eating.
- Guilt, shame and being secretive.
- Avoiding food in social situations.
- Lack of control surrounding food and eating.
- Eating a lot of food very quickly.
- Going to the toilet after eating frequently.
- Frequent over-exercising.

(NHS UK, 2020)

What are some of the noticeable physical side effects of Bulimia?

- Feeling lightheaded and in some cases fainting.
- Tooth decay and sensitivity.
- Throat swelling or sore throats.
- Dry skin.
- Scars on hands from using fingers to purge.

(Ann Pietrangelo, 2019)

WHAT CAUSES BULIMIA NERVOSA?

Although there are many environmental factors when it comes to an eating disorder, a lot of our pre-dispositions begin much deeper than surface level. Having a family history of eating disorders or even chemical changes in the brain can leave you more susceptible. People who already struggle with low self-esteem issues, perfectionism, impulsivity, past or childhood trauma and troubled relationships can all be attributed to the building blocks of an eating disorder. We typically jump to associating eating disorders due to something like bullying or hormone changes, but the reality is that eating disorders run deep for sufferers. Although they may be triggered or catalyzed by one of the above, they are not created by them. Your daughter's eating disorder may just have been lying dormant. Those self-esteem issues most likely stem from some unresolved trauma, but the list of probable causes is vast and limitlessly unique for individuals. Bullying or a similar isolated incident may have triggered this, but this has probably been in the cards for your daughter for some time. Her poor sense of self was sadly going to rear its head at some point.

Teenage girls and young women are also more at risk than men for eating disorders, but boys and men are very much still affected. Eating disorders are also more prominent in those with other underlying mental health problems. Often these are anxiety disorders, depression or obsessive-compulsive disorder. Stress can also be a risk factor, if significant or difficult change is present in the child's life this can also factor into the presence of an eating disorder. Something like a divorce, moving to a new area or losing a beloved pet can all be factors that weigh into the reasoning behind your daughter's Bulimia. Control is a key component of an eating disorder, so if your child's life is chaotic or just tougher than usual this could be the child's subconscious way of taking back some control in their lives. Much of a child's life is out of their control, so naturally the urge is typically stronger in younger sufferers. Dieting can also leave you at a higher risk of developing an unhealthy obsession, such as spending too much time thinking about losing weight or thinking about how to 'better' your appearance. Diets can easily snowball into obsessive or disordered habits and thinking patterns. Intermittent fasting, calorie counting and weighing days can all be especially problematic. A lot of diets build their foundation on tracking food intake, weight and exercise. This can be a great tool for losing weight, but it can also be a slippery slope to an eating disorder as many disorders over obsess on numbers, routines and patterns as a method of control. The control factor within diets is intended as a healthy way of managing food, but there is a fine line between this and it becoming unhealthy. (Mayo clinic, 2018)

Bullying is tragically a particularly popular culprit when it comes to triggering an eating disorder. School is tough on us all. In high school, body and hormonal changes occur at different rates and the urge to compare body types is strong. Your daughter may face the brimming pressure from boys and your peers to maintain your figure. There is suddenly a divide between those that wear padded bras and make up and those that don't. The days of running around in mixed gender groups playing tag are long gone. Image becomes an immediate dividing factor in all social settings. It can promote or demote you in an instant. This brings a mammoth amount of pressure to the school environment and many teenagers feel the need to drastically change their appearance to gain acceptance and avoid isolation from their peers. We see a lot of children rebel from this as well at this age, but many choose the simpler road of conformity. This is also the age where our sexuality is beginning to awaken, thus with it how much attention we pay to our image and to everybody else's. The attention of the opposite gender and how much of it we get is now far more important and also plays into the social side of school much more as our children's age hits double digits. The school environment is a different world to the familiarity they've known for so long. Gossiping and making jokes out of each other becomes the larger part of what the mini society of school deems discussable. Difference and diversity are largely discouraged, so it's no wonder that rates for eating disorders are particularly prevalent in our teenagers.

Even if your daughter has a wide and 'popular' social circle, this still comes with its own sense of pressure. The school hierarchy is decided by our peers after all, so even if your daughter finds herself being thrust to a high social status, it's not necessarily what she wants or a pleasant experience for her. I was a cheerleader with a boyfriend on the football team, so from the outside I seemingly had everything a high school girl could have dreamed of. This dream however was not one that was easily maintained; with it came an inescapable visibility at all times. When you are put on a pedestal, you are expected to maintain that level of perfection without fault and whilst under the watchful eyes of the other students. With that comes a crippling pressure. This criticism and pressure, for me, turned inwards as it does for so many girls. I began to spend long periods of time scrutinizing my appearance in the mirror, pinpointing areas like my thighs and stomach to check they didn't look 'fat' or unattractive. Rapidly this snowballed into me, limiting my eating, purging and binging. Before long, my body was buried beneath my clothes as my weight plummeted to 90lbs.

This pressure, as you can imagine, is greatly amplified when bullying and ridicule comes into play. Feelings of being inadequate, weird or undeserving of friends can leave our daughters feeling as though they need to take some action to change. There's no room for exceptions in the volatile social hierarchy and so your daughter feels her only option is to change herself. One of the most profound changes you can make to your body is through losing weight and unfortunately this is the first step many take down the long winding road to Bulimia Nervosa. Uniform codes at schools prevent our daughters from being able to express themselves through clothes, accessories, hair and makeup, so naturally our weight becomes the first point of call. Once the initial weight is lost and our daughters begin feeling better about themselves, a vicious and very addicting cycle is created. As we feel more comfortable and confident with our weight loss, the sufferer craves that feeling in the subconscious yet again and thus a pattern is created. Naturally, her mind seeks to re-create the actions that brought her those positive feelings. This will be even more predominant if there are disruptive, negative or stressful situations happening in her life. Plea-sure seeking is one way that we subconsciously attempt to self-soothe. Our minds are much more intelligent than we believe they are most of the time; we give them little credit for their ability to help us heal on totally unconscious levels. If your daughter has experienced something painful, she could also be seeking pleasure through her weight loss without even knowing that's what she is doing. Our brains thrive on those positive feelings, as a way of lessening or temporarily forgetting the previous pain we experienced. This doesn't mean that her actions are justifiable though, as they will still result in serious health complications if not addressed. Pleasure seeking could just be another factor to add to the ever-growing puzzle. You could look into some more positive ways of releasing those positive chemicals and hormones her brain is craving so desperately though. Hijacking her brain to receive the much-needed positive feelings from a healthier supply could make significant changes to your daughter's health. Alternatively, try suggesting she talk to her therapist about her trauma as they will be armed with the adequate skills to unpack it.

With a now dysmorphic view of themselves created in the mind, the mirror will never align with their ideal body. This will not stop the eating disorder from pushing them to continually lose weight to a dangerous extent. They are constantly chasing the point that will bring the most satisfaction but because of Bulimia's critical and skewed view on weight, your daughter will probably never be able to achieve that goal, no matter how much weight she loses. This is what leads to serious health implications for so many girls affected by Bulimia and sadly in some cases fatalities.

Social media is increasingly present in high schools and our teenagers lives and as result, is another source of huge pressure that many of us didn't have to face ourselves. This can make understanding how this affects your daughter a troubling task. Social media invites the presence of paid models, filters, editing apps, Photoshop, contouring and specialist lighting to achieve supposedly 'perfect' pictures within the comfort of your own phone. Being an 'influencer', or in other words a paid social media celebrity, is now a well-accepted and fairly common profession. However, the majority of these individuals have access to the best versions of all of those previously listed above. With the best editing software, cameras and lighting at their disposal, these individuals only influence us to hold achievable expectations of themselves and their bodies. The average teen girl can just simply not match up to this, however, they're both on the same platform and typically around the same age and thus many girls are led to believe these pictures are a real representation of how this person looks. Social media is the beauty magazine of the 2020s, and now our celebrities are in our homes and on our social media pages. There is seemingly no escape from these unrealistic expectations for our teenage girls. Their pictures are deemed worthy or unworthy by the total likes they get in comparison to these girls and their peers. If they have too few, they risk feeling insignificant and not good enough. This is something that our generation didn't have to deal with, if someone wanted to tell you that you were attractive, they had to pluck up the courage to come and tell you. Being able to like people you find appealing from the comfort of your own home, work or essentially anywhere has made our self-worth all too accessible for others to tap into. This 'liking' system attached to most social media platforms creates an addictive sense of validation and many girls sadly find much of their identity and self-worth reliant or in some way tied up in their presence on social media. With such an invasive inescapable burden on our teens, it's no wonder that they sadly feel the need to change themselves for the world around them. To be able to seem like an ordinary functioning member of society now, you need to have a social media presence of some kind, often spread out over a few different apps and webpages. Without one you risk being dubbed as a weirdo and thus people give you a slightly wider birth. This is definitely the truth for our teens, the majority of the way that they interact out of school is through social media after all. You might find it hard to imagine this or relate to it but try to imagine having to maintain several pages at once, constantly feeling the need to take pictures to make sure that they are up to date and that what you put out there is attractive or the 'best' version of yourself. The pressure behind all of that is staggering, so much more of your daughter's life is seemingly outside her control, even if she doesn't realize it. While many of us had the joy of going home and leaving our school life where it belongs, at school, our children don't have that luxury. Their school and social life follows them into their house, into their pockets and bags no matter the destination or occasion.

Social media can be utilized as a tool for so many great things, but sadly this isn't what the majority of teenagers use it for. A space for creativity, knowledge and awareness are all things that the growth of the internet has brought to us at the tap of a button. It is true that it has some fantastic uses, like anything, if it is used correctly. Perhaps having a deeper conversation with your daughter about how her social media pages have a negative impact on her could help her to realize that it is not as harmless as it seems. Let her know though that it can be used in a more effective way and be equally, if not more so, beneficial and useful for her. There's no harm in having a few pages posted about your life, blog writing can be a fun hobby, but it's when it becomes obsessive that our children struggle to separate their external and internal person. Unfortunately, this happens more often than we'd care to admit in our teenagers. They're the first generation to really go through this, and so the support is fairly non-existent by us as parents or their teachers and schools. Making it extra important to get involved if their relationship with social media is becoming more frequent, and to learn as much as you can from the internet itself and by speaking to your daughter about how this is affecting her.

2

WHY IS MY DAUGHTER MAKING HERSELF SICK?

o those without an eating disorder, the signs and symptoms can be elusive and very challenging to spot. The majority of us only pick up on changes when the eating disorder is already well under way, your daughter may have already begun purging regularly, or losing vast amounts of weight. You are most likely kicking yourself for not noticing how badly she was feeling sooner. Is important to remember that an eating disorder is a complex mental health problem that can be very unique and personal to the individual. Not only that but with a high presence of shame in this disorder, a large part of the disorder is often based on secrecy, to mask the mass of shame they feel. Thus, the sufferer feels more isolated and overwhelmed by their problems and a vicious cycle is created. You are most likely not a medical, behavior or diet professional and therefore easily misled when it comes to the signs. You've managed to recognize the issue now and are seeking knowledge, help and support for your daughter, that is the important part.

NOTICING THE SIGNS

Signs of Bulimia Nervosa can start very small, and the majority of cases are not discovered until the disorder has made very obvious changes to your child or their habits surrounding food. Some telling signs to look out for are wearing baggy clothes a lot (to hide their appearance as they have a very low self-esteem and body dysmorphia), eating rapidly, abnormally large or small portion sizes than they'd typically eat, going to the toilet for long periods of time after eating, a change in their eating habits, sticking strictly to set food routines, portion sizes and calorie intake, fears surrounding eating or an inability to stop and any negative self-talk such as "I'm fat", "I hate my body", "I wish I looked like that". (John Hopkins Medicine,2022)

It's crucial to remember that this is not a problem you can solve by simply pointing out that your child's body and weight is perfect the way it is. Your child has both a physical weight and a physiological weight, the way they seem themselves is not based on a true reflection of themselves but on the contorted version placed on them by the disorder. Only through therapy and intervention will they be able to realize this, and your seemingly helpful comments may fall on deaf ears. Try to restrain from making frustrated comments and remember that this is not out of stubbornness, unwillingness to listen or any of the other dismissive statements regularly pinned to struggling teenagers. An eating disorder is far more serious than any of the above and labeling it as such will only land your child into a more isolated and difficult position. Mental health problems are very real and very severe. With the ability to change your self-perception and skew your entire world view, this is not something that the sufferer has much control over at all. They are at the mercy of the bulimia nervosa, and they are most certainly not the driver of it. In effect they are in the passenger seat as the eating disorder drives them down the road of a poor relationship with food and their body.

In this situation many parents feel powerless to be able to help their children with such a complex and delicate topic, talking things through with them and listening to how they feel and making them feel like you understand is always helpful. Healthy communication is extra important and will help to make your child feel safe to disclose and discuss openly about their eating disorder. You should be careful not to invalidate their beliefs via the eating disorder but rather sympathize and empathize. Put yourself into their shoes and let them know that you recognize the burden this must be having on them. Talking it through with a therapist who understands the situation is also a good idea, as they will be able to give you the safest guidance on what topics to avoid or tread lightly on.

WHAT CAN YOU DO TO HELP?

Identification and awareness are the first two steps in this situation. Recognizing what your daughter is doing and being acutely aware of the severity of her condition is vital. It can be a challenge to know for sure if you have real reason to suspect an eating disorder and you may have sat tentatively on the fence of uncertainty for some time now. Eating disorders are intensely private and secretive in nature, so if you're beginning to notice possible signs you are most probably right. Bulimia takes great care in keeping itself well hidden within the sufferer and signs typically go unnoticed until some time has passed and more drastic, unavoidable changes become apparent. Writing down or making a list of the concerns that you have is a good way of tracking your thoughts. Life is nuts and so often we dismiss or forget things that we mean to hang onto and thus we innocently don't notice patterns arising. It could also help you to differentiate between genuine concerns and worrying or over-thinking situations.

With our children, we constantly want to protect them and sometimes we can over worry and project that feeling onto them a little. Looking back over what you've written at another time, with a fresh mindset, may help you to be able to see more clearly which things are significant and which are less worrisome. Talking it through with your partner, a friend or a family member that you can trust are all other good ways of getting a little footing, if you're still unsure.

Asking your daughter is not the best option until you're more sure of what is going on. She may still be cemented in her denial and struggle to understand your concern at this point. If, however, you're still seeing significant signs that she is struggling on some level with an eating disorder it is paramount that you take action to get support and advice in place as soon as possible. Research conducted in Australia found that the average lifetime of the disorder is five years, however this can be significantly longer depending on when treatment begins. When treatment is in place it is found that 45% of Bulimia patients made a full recovery and 27% made significant progress with their disordered habits and thinking patterns. (Beat Eating Disorders, 2022) The sooner that support is asked for and medical intervention is put in place, the better chance your teenager has of recovering.

So, how do you take the next step for your daughter? Next you should schedule an appointment for your child with their doctor so that they can determine whether or not your child is dealing with a diagnosable eating disorder. There are quite a few eating disorders, so they will need to ask your daughter a variety of questions to try and determine which specific disorder they are dealing with. Bulimia and anorexia are the two most common disorders but there are a few lesser-known conditions with their own unique characteristics.

There are five eating disorders recognized as diagnosable conditions in the DSM and ICD (medical manuals used by professionals) but there are a further eight disorders that mental health specialists also recognize. All of the disorders have a common denominator, that they induce harmful or fearful behaviors and thinking patterns towards food but the symptoms of each vary widely. The five recognized by doctors are Anorexia Nervosa, Bulimia Nervosa, Muscle Dysmorphia, Binge Eating Disorder and OSFED and Other specified feeding or eating disorders. Anorexia is known more commonly as it is the most potent and potentially dangerous eating disorder of the total 12. With the highest mortality rate, it combines many of the symptoms of the other disorders such as purging, calorie counting, fasting and over-exercising in one very complex and terrifying disorder. (Breathe life healing center, 2021)

This is not to say that the other disorders are secondary and all of the above should be treated with the same seriousness as anorexia. Each disorder comes with its own challenges, symptoms and thought patterns although similarities and crossovers do occur. Regardless, a medical professional is your best port of call once you are more sure that your suspicions and fears about your daughter's eating are true. Online research is beneficial to your daughter, but you are not going to be able to fix this alone. Attempting to 'fix' your daughter's eating issues at home is incredibly dangerous and **should not** be attempted. The costs to your daughter's recovery time, and overall mental and physical health is too high to risk missing out on excellent advice and support. If you're worried about seeing a doctor because you're ashamed, embarrassed or have a negative view of medical practitioners as a whole then you need to leave your predispositions and opinions at the door for the sake of your child. There is no amount of "can do" attitude and certainty that can outweigh years of professional training and on the job experience inside the medical field. Your daughter's disorder is nothing to be ashamed of, this is something completely outside of her control. Would you refuse her medical care for another kind of serious illness simply to save your own ego or 'reputation'? If your daughter was walking around with a broken leg, would you rush her to hospital or hide her away for other people's benefit?

While it's understandable that an eating disorder is a hard thing for you to come to terms with, particularly if you haven't been educated or experienced them before in your lifetime, you have a responsibility and duty of care to the little girl with the serious illness. If you are of the older generation or have parents or close family who are speaking negatively of your daughter's issues, it's understandable that you may have been raised with incorrect views of people with mental health conditions. We are human and are allowed to get things wrong, we've not all been raised with the tools we need to cope with the world as we may have grown up in a less accepting society with different moral values. Just because this is a mental health illness does not mean it is any less real or severe than something visibly obvious. Other people's opinions should also be totally irrelevant when your child is in a dangerous position and potentially at risk. Just because your parents or peers your age may struggle to understand Bulimia, does not mean that you have to follow suit. Remaining ignorant or inconsiderate is not excusable. A brief adjustment period is all that is needed, as well as some education, knowledge and support on the subject.

A medical professional will also be able to assess for any other physical complications as a result of the eating disorder. Eating disorders come with a whole plethora of after-the-fact issues as a whole and Bulimia is the most prolific disorder when it comes to knock on physical effects. These vary in severity from fatigue, irregular or absent periods, fits and muscle spasms, heart, kidney and bowel problems, osteoporosis and other bone related problems. (NHS, 2022) The longer the bulimia and the other health issues are left untreated the worse the repercussions become, so getting your child to a medical professional and getting them up to speed on the situation is critical to your child's recovery and overall health and wellbeing.

Your doctor will discuss the next steps and treatment programs available and be a guide for you on getting your child the best help that they can get. The help that your teen will receive will depend greatly on the severity of your daughter's situation and how much damage the eating disorder has already caused and how strongly it has a hold over her. If she is in the earlier stages and has not yet broken through the denial stage, she may need significant work from a talk therapist. If she has recognized a problem but is unsure how to change her habits, she will need guidance on how to take those steps safely and comfortably. Typically, a qualified therapist will guide your daughter through a self-help book that will strategically work through the different parts of an eating disorder and the mindset behind it. They'll most likely ask your daughter to keep an eating log, set some more realistic meal goals and help your daughter work to meet them. A therapist will also attempt to pinpoint the triggers for your daughter and what things she and her family can do to prevent her being triggered in the future.

If, however, it is felt that your daughter is in immediate danger or in a place where a more 'hands-on' method of support is needed then she may be offered in-patient care at a mental health center for young people. Although this is a scary thought for many parents and for the teen involved, this step could be the difference between you having a daughter and not having one. In addition, this could possibly be the beginning of opening up a new world and a new lease of life for your daughter.

In-patient care is rare and often is only utilized until the young person has made some change or positive steps in the right direction, think of it as a leg up onto the right path. This could mean your child would be supervised at all times while eating and would have round the clock care and support to give her the best chance at fighting the monster that is Bulimia. This kind of support could be world-changing and get her strongly walking down the road to recovery.

These individuals are often specially trained in their field and deal with eating disorder patients exclusively and on a regular basis. If anybody is qualified and best equipped to help your daughter, it is the teams that work tirelessly inside the inpatient care units. They offer unique and specific care to each individual to help everyone make the most progress that they can.

This could vary from observing her eat a whole meal or going with her to the toilet to ensure she doesn't purge; they will work all hours to help young people walk the road of recovery and make sure that they are not doing it alone. This could be sitting up with her in the night to prevent her from binging and instead offer her a healthier alternative and some company while she does so. She'll also have the opportunity to make friends in her age group that live in her area, with similar problems to herself. Being surrounded by others like herself, will help to take some of the pressure off your teenager and let her release some of the shame she may feel.

As you begin to spiral into your disordered habits, the less normal you feel, so being surrounded by other teens in her position may help to lessen the abnormality she might otherwise feel. These other teenagers also understand how each other is feeling, they are all at the center for the same or similar reasons, this will give her a group of understanding young people to talk to when she is having troubles or worries. Sometimes an adult can be off putting to talk to, as there is obviously an age barrier present, and some adults struggle to empathize with teens and young children.

Other teens on the other hand will be able to relate to a lot of her life issues and problems, such as dealing with the social hierarchy of school. You might be worried about bullying being a factor inside the inpatient area itself. Staff members are also there to deal with any social issues that arise and help mediate and put boundaries in place where needed. Their jobs don't begin and end at medical care, they also play the role of caregiver while your child is away from you, so they carry the same duty of care as any parent or carer would.

Isolation from their child is another fear that many parents have regarding inpatient care. Being away from your child can never be an easy thing and no matter their destination you will always worry about them, that's your caring role and it is not something that you can switch off. Sibling separation is something that runs alongside this concern too as many parents worry what temporarily splitting up their children will do to each child and the family as a whole. Visiting hours are normally daily in these centers and children have access to use the phone to call too. Some offer children to return home at weekends or holidays too.

Some centers allow patients to use their cell phones too while others have stricter policies that deem social media etc. to be too much of a trigger for some patients. Everything discussed depends largely on what your local center is like. You may want to consider going for a visit around your nearest inpatient care unit and voicing your concerns. If you're unhappy with your local center, there is always the option to travel to another area and see if the latter is more suited to you and your daughter's needs. Ultimately, it is about what is best for your daughter and what will help her get to a better point. Once your daughter has made some progress, she could be well enough to come home anyway. Most inpatient stays are fairly temporary and long periods of time spent in inpatient care are pretty rare.

Whatever treatment your daughter is given, the road will be emotionally draining for you and her. Being there for her as someone to offer non-judgmental support and positivity is really all you can do. For the most part you are sadly a bystander. Learning as much and gaining as much informative knowledge as possible about Bulimia is another great step to take. Knowledge is powerful and, in this situation, the more you have the better you can offer advice and support to your daughter.

This will show your daughter you're making a conscious decision to understand how she feels, and you'll be able to give a deeper level of support with the more insight and information that you have in your tool belt. Empathy, consideration and care will all make a huge difference to your teen so simply being there as a person with compassion and understanding can help lift some of the pressure and judgment she feels from the world. She may be growing up and becoming a more complex individual, but she is still the little girl that begged to cuddle you when she was small, talked your ear off about her interests and made you laugh so hard your ribs hurt at her 'creative' and questionable crayon masterpieces as a toddler.

She is and always will be, your little girl. Her problems may be bigger than scraped knees now, but she still needs you to be there. Our children never outgrow their need for love and support, the way they need it just changes as they grow. They may need you seemingly less but when they do for bigger issues, this is just a sign that you have nurtured and raised an independent teen who will one day be an independent adult.

3

SHE JUST WANTS ATTENTION

*T*ragically, when it is discovered that their daughter has Bulimia or a similar eating disorder, many teachers, parents and friends write this off as an attempt to gain attention. There's no doubt that there are teenage girls, boys and even adults out there who feel the need to create lies to gain attention from others, we've all ran into these kinds of people in our lifetime. These individuals however are rare and reasonably easy to identify. Needing validation and attention constantly from outside sources is a problematic self-esteem issue in itself and one that should also be talked about. Ridicule invites shame and isolation, in any situation that is unhealthy in a person. A child will also no doubt carry this sad ideology with them through to adulthood. Bulimia Nervosa on the other hand, has absolutely nothing to do with attention of any sort. This eating disorder thrives on the existence of shame, it is so tightly woven into the core of Bulimia. Attention is the last thing someone struggling with Bulimia wants. This is a child who has a very damaged sense of self-worth and is trying to continually 'better' themselves using harmful methods and practices.

Many parents choose to believe this is the simplicity of their daughter's situation surrounding food as a way of escaping the hard realities of having a daughter with Bulimia. This attempt to rid themselves of parental guilt and avoid acknowledging the severity of the scenario is incredibly destructive to the mental health of a young girl affected with a potentially life-threatening mental health condition. Not only does this annihilate a large portion of her support system but it diminishes and denies her true and very vulnerable feelings. Shame and isolation are a lethal combination when it comes to Bulimia and her parents' behavior will ultimately cause the situation to escalate dramatically.

I myself have never received an official diagnosis, as when I voiced my concerns to my parents, they rolled their eyes and dismissed my attempt to seek help and advice as a cry for attention. I only realized what I was experiencing when reading through a textbook in a high school psychology class, the symptoms of Anorexia and Bulimia aligned perfectly with what I had been enduring for the last few years, yet my parents failed to take action.

One day I felt my heart start racing and I was struggling to breathe when I was sitting in class, it wasn't a panic attack as there was no existing stress etc., but a cry for help from my body and thankfully this time I listened. I decided to try and make some change, without the support of my family. Seemingly they had accepted my skeletal appearance and did nothing to even recognize my strikingly obvious concerns. The closest my family ever came to addressing my disorder was when another parent attending an afterschool football game mentioned to my mom that I was looking 'a little' thin, my mom later questioned me if I was trying to lose weight to which I obviously said no, and the conversation ceased to appear again.

You might wonder why I said that I wasn't trying to lose weight, as it would obviously appear that I was, but eating disorders are formed from a negative sense of self, not because the sufferer wants to lose weight. They simply remain stuck, at the mercy of their disorder. I was left completely isolated and alone with my problems, seemingly abandoned by my family. Obviously, this made making any recovery or positive steps that bit harder, but thankfully, I persevered and fought hard to regain a better relationship with food. Recovery is possible, but it is tough so remember both.

Of course, beneath our parental status we are still people of our own, with emotions that often get caught in life's crossfire. Possibly one of the most challenging aspects in your role as parent is keeping calm and collected in times of high stress or emotion and acting as a buffer between your children and the harder parts of our world. When you're struggling or feeling overwhelmed, remember what the damage of the opposite could do. If you have emotional outbursts or offload onto them without care for how it will make them feel you risk exposing them to trauma and making them feel as though they need to internalize their feelings for the sake of others.

Our childhoods are our building blocks for life. How our parents handle tough situations is in turn how we will later in life. This doesn't mean lock your feelings away and throw away the key, instead remain self-aware and keep open communication with your daughter. You're setting the measure to which she will continually weigh herself against for life, bare that in mind. Sharing any similar past experience with eating disorders or low esteem can also help to let your daughter know that nobody goes through life without some issues of their own along the way. It'll also demonstrate to her that it's okay to talk about these things and there is no reason to feel ashamed about the way she feels. If there is one really useful tool you can give your daughter to help her, being a place of safety, security, openness, trust and guidance is one of the best things you can be.

EMOTIONAL EXPLOSIONS

One of the lesser discussed symptoms of Bulimia, mood swings and emotional outbursts are not typically what we associate with an eating disorder. Regardless they are a prevalent factor, particularly in teenagers who are already undergoing significant hormonal changes. They can be distressing and frustrating for teens and their families. With the already sensitive topic of Bulimia, it can be difficult to know how to navigate these as a parent without risking your child's wellbeing in the process. These mood swings often come across as anger, irritability, impatience and deep sadness. (Life works, 2021) This is as a result of two factors: a poor mental state and physical exhaustion or lack of energy from the strain of going from binging to purging again and again. Bulimia takes a great toll on the body and mind. With much of the sufferers' time spent thinking negatively about themselves or trying to navigate their way through life with a growing fear-based relationship with food, it's evident where this mental exhaustion is coming from. Alongside your body constantly being forced to expel and take in large quantities of food, while also fighting to keep all systems running. Your body is a vast and complicated machine to keep running, with so many different areas needing fuel it's no wonder that our body's struggle to run on the bare minimum. We're simply not biologically equipped to handle the effects of an eating disorder long term and the result can lead to great damage to our body.

Food is after all a fairly unavoidable foe to have. With most families sitting down together for at least one meal a day and eating in the company of friends at school, the social pressure and inability to escape from the fear can have a draining and detaching effect on the individual. Constantly being empty, starving and uncomfortable is a draining cycle for the body to have to undergo on such a regular basis. Combined with the earlier discussed pressures that are present in high school. The ever-watching eyes of the sea of teenagers makes keeping any kind of secret incredibly challenging. Imagine carrying that burden that you have a secret that could at any moment be found out alongside the draining feeling of being burnt out?

Talking to your child's school about their Bulimia would also be another great step to take. Getting them some kind of support person in place would help deduct from the towering number of fears and stresses already on your teenagers back. This could be in the form of a tutor, guidance counselor, or just a favorite teacher that they feel comfortable disclosing information to. Involve your child in the conversation about support and try to make it work for them. It's no good having their head of year assigned as a supporting member of staff if your daughter doesn't feel comfortable talking to her. Taking some positive control of the situation in this way, is a really strong step for your teen to have made too and will no doubt go towards helping her down the road to recovery.

Attention is really the last thing someone with Bulimia nervosa wants. Even if your daughter is typically confident and maybe even popular at school, too much attention causes teens to gain an incredibly critical perception of self. This feeling of being watched and admired puts a weight of expectations on the backs of our children, as it would to anyone. When you have a large peer and friend group that idolizes you and continually looks up to you for guidance, it can be hard to not transfer the same standards and expectations onto yourself. High school truly is one of the toughest times we go through in our lifetime, so much is learnt and so much trauma ensues and yet it's a topic rarely talked about. Our teenage years are one of the most rapid times of change for our bodies, minds and our lives. We enter as a child and leave as a young adult ready to make the next steps in their lives. Your next steps for life rely solely on your ability to perform the tasks set in front of you and to retain the knowledge you are force-fed. Coupled with peer pressure, so much of our teens' lives are out of control. It should come as no surprise why the minds of our teens fall prey to Bulimia and the obsessive control it brings.

ENVIRONMENTAL EFFECTS

While Bulimia brings a whole host of shame and self-hate, we rarely hear about the parts of this disorder that make our daughters feel 'good'. If there were no perceived 'positives', then why would our children be doing this to themselves? It is the positive feelings that ensnares our daughters. Once they are trapped, escaping the pattern is a much more challenging task, especially for one person alone and unaided. That's before you factor in shame, guilt and fear of ridicule. Our daughters spend the majority of their time chasing the gratifying and accomplished feeling's that come alongside the actual weight loss itself. Weight loss and the ability to change your appearance come with a rush of satisfaction. When we succeed at something, and we make perceived positive change we fuel our brain with positive feelings and chemicals that it will subconsciously seek to recreate. Alternatively, they feel the same hate and self-loathing that they have felt before and feel helpless to change the self that they dislike so passionately. The rush is incredibly temporary though, as once purging and other disordered acts begin, more and more shame swamp her emotions. In turn, re-igniting her self-hate.

This is why jokes; whether by family, friends or a comedian on the tv, surrounding eating disorders, fat, weight or appearance can be so damaging for the young girl struggling with Bulimia. You could be passing comments on a stranger in the street, or someone you know well or dislike, the context is irrelevant to the self-conscious girl who will absorb any forms of criticism and use them to measure herself against. While these jokes can be funny and light-hearted in the presence of stable and self-secure adults, the same cannot be said for children and teenagers. Particularly if they are already struggling with low self-esteem or an eating disorder. Children and teens are like sponges to their environment, so although it may feel strange to not make simple off-hand comments like the above; it can be world altering for the life of your children. What and who you have around your children will shape what they find acceptable in later life and what they don't. Beginning to pay more atten-tion to what your children are exposed to, however small, is another productive thing you can do to help your daughter. Heartbreakingly, many children in neglectful or dysfunc-tional backgrounds unfortunately go on to live challenging and complicated lives. Disturbed early brain development as a direct result of being maltreated can actually cause physical impairments to the brain's functions and ability to perform. Memory, self-control and cognitive flexibility are all affected by the events surrounding the child in childhood. (Child Welfare Information Gateway, 2019)

While you may not feel as though your children have been exposed to trauma directly, trauma is largely perspective dependent. Meaning that what you perceive as being traumatic, someone else may not or the opposite. While you may not think that you are passing on any traumatic or problematic habits, worries or experiences onto your children, you may well be. I have personal experience of this from my teenage years too. In the midst of my struggle with Bulimia my family went out for a nice meal at a restaurant, it was the perfect setting for a pleasant family evening. My father, however, passed a comment that has survived in my memories through to adulthood. He called me a "bone rack" and started laughing. I failed to see the humor in his remark, all I could feel was the pain and the further self-hate that it brought about. To many this may have been an offhand comment or a bad joke, but to me it was deeply painful at a time when I already felt vulnerable.

Many past generations of parents were ignorant to the true emotions connected to many of the parenting methods and situations that they put our parents and grandparents in, we tend to go with whatever is most socially acceptable of the time. Society is notoriously bad for changing its mind though and doing it often. While for the most part society grows for the better, we cannot be sheep and follow blindly, because it is not us but our children that will be led to the wolves.

Being honest with yourself, optimistic to change and self-aware of how you interact with your teen and the way you interact with their world can go a long way. Our kids are just growing people at the end of the day; we've all been through it. A little humility can go a long way to raising a secure and confident child. Finding that balance with exposure is a mountainous feat and it's likely we won't ever do as well as we feel we should, but giving it our best go is all we can do. Our daughters are only this young once. They have decades of adulthood ahead of them and only really two as your child, so make the most of it and make it a time you can both be happy and proud of. Being young is about enjoying life while you've got the energy to! What a waste it would be to toss those years away in favor of carelessness and ease.

REMOVING WEIGHT FROM THE EQUATION

It can be tricky to know how to encourage healthy eating habits and discourage and prevent disordered eating within your teen. Finding the fine line between helpful and harmful as a parent can feel impossible. One important thing to remember is that life is fluid and flexible, we simply don't stay the same way forever. Change is an unavoidable part of life. Your teen may be struggling with their eating at this moment in time and may even have previously received a Bulimia diagnosis from a doctor, but this is not a death sentence that they must carry with them for eternity. We change and grow in our lifetimes, sometimes we slip into a bad patch or adopt some temporary bad and even dangerous habits, but it can change. Many children go through a variety of phases and stages with their eating naturally as they grow, and their appetite needs and tastes change. Problems usually only start to occur when pressure and food join forces. We also accidentally teach our children to ignore their stomach a lot of the time, which can result in disordered eating down the line. Forcing children to eat all their food at mealtimes even when they don't want to is a very common one. Although most of us think we have our child's best interests at heart, they stop listening to their body when it tells them they are full. Equally if you don't allow your children food when they ask for snacks, they'll learn to ignore hunger.

These problematic behaviors will not raise their head until later on when the little girl has become a teenager who is now disconnected from her nutritional needs. So, remember, just at the moment your daughter's relationship with food has indeed changed, but it most probably will again. She may have adopted some harmful habits but what has been done can be undone again. What matters is what you do now to give her the best chance of getting better.

Our teens' relationship with food could also have changed to be used as a kind of self-soothing or comfort seeking activity. This in its simplest form is a relatively normal thing. We've all had that crappy day and come home to mope on the sofa with the comfort of our dear friends: ice cream, pizza and chocolate. This is a healthy and completely 'normal' way to self-soothe with food. This typically occurs once in a blue moon when our daughters are feeling down on life. If, however this is beginning to occur more often, or is woven into a "food routine" then it is indeed another part of disordered eating. Food can be enjoyed without our children feeling the need to frequently use it as an emotional crutch. Our problems begin here. Once your child has binged on junk food to soothe themselves, they will soon be hit with a wave of guilt, regret and shame, and the dark inner voice of the eating disorder will come out to push them to purge. One way to stop this from happening is to recognize the earlier signs and stop the cycle before it has become entrenched in our daughter's way of living. Checking in with your daughter regularly and giving her the opportunity to talk whatever is bothering her through with you will help remind her that there are other opportunities for support and comfort. A hug, taking a walk or drive together or letting her pick a movie for you both to watch can all be healthier ways for you to help her to soothe. Our mind's feed on patterns and repetitions, so helping to break those and then replace them with more positive habits is a fantastic way of preventing the end result.

Doing this is challenging however, as teens with eating disorders consider their disordered actions to be a solution to the way they are feeling, so don't be discouraged if it takes a little while for your daughter to take you up on the offer. (Young Minds,2022) Giving her the time and space to make the decision for herself will reduce pressure on her, and stop her from feeling like you're on her back rather than trying to help. You could try suggesting activities and phrasing it like you're asking her to tag along, rather than going out of your way to do something directly for her. Again, this will decrease pressure in the situation. Some ways of phrasing this could be:

- "I feel like going for a walk, we haven't walked the trails in ages! Would you like to come along?"
- "I might go grab a few things from the store and then go for a drive, do you want to come and keep me company?"
- "I'm really in the mood for the beach, do you want to come with me if I go on Saturday?"

You can also help your teenager to self-soothe alone by suggesting some healthier ways of doing so and getting them some things to get them started. If you think your teen would enjoy journaling then why not go the extra mile and get them a really nice journal, pens, coloring pencils and stickers? If your teen loves art, why not book them a painting class or buy them a few canvases and some paints to get going? For the more outdoorsy girl, why not book her a horse-riding lesson? Treat her to some quality equestrian

SHANNON MICHELLE

equipment like a riding hat in her favorite color! Taking the first steps for her and making her feel important to you could be the things that give her the little nudge she needs to get started at a potentially life-saving new way of self-soothing. Creativity and nature are both brilliant places to start when channeling that excess negative energy into something practical or creative. A new rewarding outlet for her emotions could give her a whole new sense of confidence and stability.

CHALLENGES YOU MAY FACE

For your teen, one of the biggest hurdles to overcome will be realizing and accepting that she has a problem with food and her perception of self. This can be incredibly challenging, as their disordered habits feel like a solution to a very real and pressing problem. With an already poor self-esteem, it's heartbreakingly easy for your daughter to believe she needs to change herself rather than accept who and what she is. Overcoming this obstacle will call upon a great deal of patience, consideration and understanding from you as a parent. They are not purposefully challenging or trying to disagree with you, they are just completely certain in their thinking. Within them another voice is convincing them constantly that their disordered habits are completely valid and that they NEED to continue them, or their weight will spiral out of control. With it their happiness too. The longer she has 'successfully' lived with her Bulimic habits, the more embedded in her they will be. Your daughter will feel safe, secure and comfortable with her routine catered to Bulimia. Everything outside of that will feel alien and very uncomfortable.

Trying to discuss this with your teenager will require a certain amount of skill, as you attempt to shine the light on the negative impact her actions are having to her body, without making her feel like you are blaming her or putting more pressure onto her to be better. As she is already suffering drastically with low self-worth, these kinds of assumptions that feel like a far jump to you, are very easy for her to make. Avoid intervention type conversations. Sitting her down and trying to force her to see what she is blindly doing to herself will not make her change. You only risk pushing her further away. It may be easier to seize the opportunity to start a conversation when the topic naturally arises. Take time to listen to how she is feeling and appreciate her point of view, while neutrally suggesting some more positive ways of handling a situation or feeling that is bubbling up. Keep the whole conversation low pressure and low demand on her end, you're just trying to give her an alternative perspective and leave it with her to think over, not to force on her. The quieter approach should leave her feeling less hassled or pressured by your thoughts and comments whilst also not dodging an important conversation.

Triggers

Learning her triggers and knowing what things affect your daughter is a very useful tool for any parent and daughter relationship but is especially helpful when mental health issues come into the picture. What does an eating disorder trigger look like? We've heard triggers spoken about in other disorders such as Post Traumatic Stress Disorder or Anxiety. Although the same rough concept applies, an ED trigger can be slightly different and sometimes trickier to pinpoint. A trigger by definition describes an event that causes an extreme or overwhelming emotional or physical reaction in the suffering individual. This is normally not a direct cause of the eating disorder, but it can be the cause behind an otherwise seemingly unnecessary or drastic response. If your teenager does not learn to manage these, she will most likely develop unhealthy and problematic coping mechanisms. These will only worsen the initial issue as your daughter's triggers and fears will only grow.

Paying closer attention to her feelings, moods and disordered habits will help you to piece together a connection. Simply starting a conversation about it will help you to gain insight into not only what things trigger her but also what being triggered feels like and means for her. You can also talk to her doctor or her therapist about these and they will be able to give you some insight from a medical point of view. It's important to remember that every sufferer of an eating disorder is different and there isn't a 'one size fits all' guide for the vast majority of ED symptoms. Your daughter may have very individual and unique triggers for her, but knowledge is power and the more you know the more aware you can be.

That said, what are some typical triggers to watch out for?

- Talking about food.
- Talking about calories.
- Commenting on portion or plate sizes.
- Talking about weight loss.
- Pictures of idealistic body types (typically celebrities).
- Stress.
- Being asked to eat in a strange place.
- Changes in her typical eating routine.
- Comments on weight (even when talking about Tv characters).

(SupportED,2022)

Your daughter could identify with all of the above triggers or none of them, talking to her and letting her be vulnerable about what possible triggers for her could be will give you an excellent insight as well as letting your daughter know you are trying your best to help her. She may not realize yet that she has triggers, so silently observing and keeping watch can help you to identify them. Research is another productive thing you can do to help educate yourself. Books like this are an excellent tool and there are a whole host of informative and supportive websites, blogs and forums available for free for both parents of children with Bulimia and the struggling teen herself. If you do suspect she has a trigger and hasn't realized, talk to your teen and their doctor or therapist. They will be able to shed light on the likelihood of that certain event being a trigger and suggest some healthy coping mechanisms. It can be tough knowing how much exposure to a trigger is too much, so it's best to seek professional advice on this. While working through triggers is advised, over exposure is unhealthy too. Your teen will not recover if you force her into too many uncomfortable situations, it's all about the balance. It's important that she feels in control of this too and that she knows her feelings are respected. As a parent you are a guide and support system, you're not there to wave a wand to make her problems disappear. For some parents taking a backseat is difficult but your teenager will soon be an adult and if you aren't already, then you will have to adjust to letting them have their own opinions, feelings and thoughts at some point. Recovery cannot be rushed, as much as we want this pain to be over for our daughter, we do not have the power to do this for her. All a parent can do in this situation is be the best kind of support system they can, in whatever way that looks for your daughter.

4

SHE NEEDS MEDICAL HELP

*G*etting medical attention for your daughter is not a negotiable option. Your teenager needs medical intervention no matter what stage she is at with the eating disorder, help is an absolute must. The earlier the medical and therapeutic attention is received, the stronger the fight that you and your daughter can put up against Bulimia. Medical professionals are also equipped with the adequate skills and knowledge to assess your daughter's situation. They will also be able to recognize any signs or symptoms of a decline in her mental or physical health and put measures in place to put your daughter into a safer position. Spotting this with an untrained eye is a monumental task, making getting professionals involved a fundamental step to aid both yourself and your daughter. You're not in this alone either, there are plenty of well qualified people out there to support and help you in this fragile situation.

It can, however, be a more difficult task convincing and getting your daughter to receive the help she needs. Even more so if she is still struggling to recognize her disordered habits as a problem. It may be an idea to make a doctor aware of her situation even if she is not prepared to talk to them herself yet. You could raise this idea with her as a kind of "first step" for her. Although there is little practical medical help a doctor can give to your daughter without meeting her directly, they will be able to advise and guide you on how to handle this situation as a parent. It will give you someone to rely on for reliable and unbiased support, somewhere to go with any concerns and thoughts, and when the time comes that your daughter feels comfortable going to see them, they will already understand her situation. This will make it easier for the doctor to be able to do most of the talking, and ask questions catered to her personal experiences and feelings. Most of the fears surrounding talking to an outside person is how to word and explain personal things, so a doctor who's already aware of the details will be a great relief to your daughter.

If she has recognized her habits or has even agreed to receive treatment, it is likely still an incredibly daunting prospect for her to be open and vulnerable with a complete stranger. Remember this at all times. You could try talking through what things she needs to talk about and how she wants to word them before going in to see the doctor, so that you're both clear on what you want to get across. Going in with her and helping her to get her points and feelings across, or just as a silent support to hold her hand will go a long way. Having someone unconditionally in your corner is a severely underrated thing, it is the greatest tool you can give your daughter in this situation. Friends will come and go but parents last a lifetime.

Many parents may think that their daughters' Bulimia is a phase. This is far from the case. While we grow and change throughout our lifetime and an eating disorder can be recovered from, it is not something that will "go away on its own". Bulimia is a serious disorder that needs treatment. Leaving it untreated will only cause the eating disorder to take greater control and spiral to dangerous levels and leave your daughter in a very dangerous and isolated position.

What are the health risks of Bulimia if it goes untreated?

Heart and blood problems

When your body does not have the sufficient calories, it needs just to keep your body fueled for everyday life, it burns the fat and muscle tissue (stores) you already have to use as fuel. Continuous exposure to a low-calorie diet or periods of being hungry or empty takes a hard toll on your heart as the whole body is put on 'power saving mode'. This makes it nearly impossible to maintain a healthy blood pressure level. Left untreated and unnoticed, it can lead to low blood pressure, fatigue, fainting and in some cases heart failure. Purging or abusing laxatives strips the body of essential electrolytes that are needed for healthy muscle function. This also decreases the correct functioning of the heart and can cause serious issues for the whole body.

Gastrointestinal problems

Our natural gastrointestinal cycle works on a schedule of digestion and expulsion. When an eating disorder is present, this natural cycle is thrown completely to the wind. Interrupted by invasive forms of expelling food and long periods of time without eating or being empty, the natural digestive cycle is in disarray. Bacterial infections, stomach discomfort, nausea and struggling to digest food are all additional effects caused by the disordered habits of Bulimia. Constipation is also a very real issue for those with eating disorders, as there is an altogether lack of enough food to progress digestion naturally.

Neurological effects

To most people's surprise Bulimia and many eating disorders bring severe complications to the brain and our neurology. Your brain, like any other part of your anatomy needs energy to function well and the implications for a brain starved of energy are often non-reversible. Dying neurons and decreased brain volume are both terrifying risks for people with an eating disorder. Seizures, numbness in the extremities and even dementia have all been found to link back to the long-term effects of an eating disorder.

Effects on the Endocrine systems

Being malnourished does great damage to our endocrine system. Drastic hormonal shifts are the first step down a long and winding road of health complications. Thyroid problems are as a direct result of fluctuating hormones. The thyroid is ultimately the hub for all hormone regulation and knocking it into disarray is dangerous and often irreversible. A sustained drop in hormones also leads to changes in bone density, strength and in some cases causes Osteoporosis. Puberty is often the first thing that sparks an eating disorder as in both girls and boys it is the beginning of a great hormonal shift. Eating disorders can also be responsible for lowering testosterone and estrogen levels and therefore disrupting normal development in teens. The hormonal imbalances previously discussed can even result in infertility. This can be both temporary or permanent depending on the severity of the damage done to the hormonal components of the reproductive system.

Sleep issues

Sleep apnea and trouble sleeping in general are both tied to eating disorders. Sufferers may find sleeping difficult if they are intensely hungry after purging sessions or if they are full and bloated after a binging session.

Death

Fatality is tragically high in eating disorders and is stagger-ingly higher than many other mental health conditions. As all of the above health conditions are a risk either at once or simultaneously the body struggles greatly to carry all of its new ailments especially with depleting nutrition and energy. Unfortunately for many young girls, help is not administered fast enough, and their eating disorder consumes them and their life. (Seeds Of Hope,2022)

While all of the above is terrifying to think about in relation to the health of your daughter, know that there most certainly is hope. With support from her family and medical professionals, there is no doubt that your daughter can make a full and lasting recovery. Being educated and aware of what the future could hold though, will help you to remain vigi-lant and aware of the possibilities. Bulimia and eating disor-ders as a whole are often overlooked and disregarded despite there being such serious health risks to the individual sufferer. Arming yourself with the knowledge of the harsh realities, however hard it may be, is vital to your role in your daughter's recovery.

DENIAL

As discussed previously in other chapters, your daughter's denial of her actions is one of the hardest steps to overcome on her recovery journey. Some parents hope that this issue resolves itself and leave their daughters to "figure it out". A partly understandable reaction to a frustrating and time sensitive situation, this is not a practical or helpful long-term solution and can be very harmful. Your daughter will not "get over it" if left unaided, if anything she will most likely grow more certain in her thinking. So how can we help our daughters to see through denial and realize the truth without pushing them away? Gently pointing out some of your daughter's behaviors when she brings them up or when an opportunity arises is the best way to go about raising the subject.

You could also explain why she might be feeling the need to do what she is doing; this will show her you've taken the time to consider how she feels. Make sure to word and express yourself in a way that shows that the way she is thinking is totally understandable but problematic long term. Some handy phrases could be:

- "I understand how you feel, but this isn't a healthy habit for you or your body"
- "I understand why you feel the need to purge, but there are other options and they'll be much safer and healthier for you. I have your back through this."
- "I know you feel the need to do this right now, but long term this is not a practical decision for your body and at some point we're going to have to try some alternatives."

SHANNON MICHELLE

Phrases like these keep the pressure off your daughter making an immediate change but still keep the focus on changing the habits when she's ready. Be prepared for her to make progress and then regress back into her previous habits. Taking on Bulimia's thought process is incredibly hard and progress is not necessarily linear. Keep doing what you're doing and offering honest but understanding advice to your daughter. A therapist is your best bet of breaking down how your daughter is feeling and on giving her some gentle insight and reasoning. Therapists are trained to try and un-pick how our brains think and why they are thinking that way, in this situation they are the best person for the job. Between you and your daughter's therapist, your daughter has at least two positive people shedding light on the realities of her actions in a respectful way. If she feels that she can talk openly to you despite you disagreeing with some of what she says then you're probably in a very good space for growth. Keeping the channels of communication open between you and your teen is half the battle when your teen is struggling with being in denial, so if she is still happy disclosing without much prompting then you're nailing it! Time is another big factor in your daughter realizing the severity of her actions. Ultimately no one can force her to believe anything that she doesn't want to, so patience and allowing her to take her time (so long as it's agreed as safe by her doctor) is probably your best bet at the moment. If, however, your teenager's condition has already significantly deteriorated then your doctor may discuss with you the benefits of in-patient care. This could end up ultimately being against your daughter's will if she is still in denial at a more pressing stage. This is a decision no parent wants to face, but in this situation you are faced with keeping your daughter happy or losing her more permanently.

GROUP THERAPY

For some teens, talking to a medical professional is too daunting, although group therapy is always available as a secondary option. Group therapy has a much more relaxed atmosphere and the attention of the leader of the session is split between multiple other teens rather than being all on your daughter. Talking 1 on 1 with an adult can be a struggle for some teens and they may find it easier to open up around others their own age. Unfortunately, sometimes there is a bit of a generation barrier between adults and teens and this can cause misunderstandings or leave teenagers feeling as though they aren't really being understood. This doesn't discredit lone therapy though, as many therapy practitioners are highly trained in their area and profession. It largely depends on your daughter and what she is the most comfortable with. The opposite can also be true, some teens find an adult more relatable.

One on one therapy with a stranger can be very scary, even more so when the topic is so personal. Denial may be something that your daughter has only recently discovered or is still dealing with, so this can add to the reluctance to discuss something so personal with a stranger. Group therapy is an especially excellent tool for girls suffering with Bulimia or a binge eating disorder but has been found to be less useful for girls with anorexia as they tend to feel a need to compete with others within the group to be thinner. Group therapy has a mass of benefits including; realizing they are not alone in their thoughts and consequent actions, friendships can be formed with supportive and like-minded individuals and identifying unhealthy behaviors is made far easier with a group that understands. Group therapy gives the girls a safe space away from the rest of their world. There is now a group of other young people that they can rely on and be completely open with, knowing that they will understand. For someone suffering with Bulimia at a time when they're in such a judgmental environment so frequently (school), this can be a complete game changer. For many parents, it's also a great weight off their backs knowing that your daughter has not just one person but a circle of people that she can talk openly with. (MentalHealth.net, 2022)

Group therapy brings your daughter an opportunity to gain real world knowledge about her disorder and others, from other young people. Talking openly about their individual experiences will expose your daughter to other possible triggers and symptoms that she may not have experienced yet and that she can look out for. It could also be an eye-opening experience if some of the other teens are further down the road than she is. This will give her a real-life view on where she is heading if her disordered habits are not changed and the impact it has had on that person and their life. If denial is still something your daughter is battling with then meeting others in her position, or worse, could be enough to pull her into the realities of her situation. Group therapy encourages each participant to talk as much or as little as they like but gives them the all-important chance to speak if they would like to. While they are speaking, they know they are being listened to and respected in the same way everybody else at the session is. Pressure is at an all-time low in a scenario like this, and any interaction is done at the complete control and will of the participants. It also levels the playing field totally and equality for all at the session, irrespective of any other factors, is fundamental. Group leaders may try to encourage conversation slightly but generally do not push anyone to speak should they not want to. If your daughter is having a rough day and doesn't feel like doing much more than listening, then that is all she needs to do! Showing up and being a listening pair of ears can be as powerful as talking sometimes.

A lot can be learned about ourselves and our own feelings when we listen to others. Your daughter may not have even let herself see and feel how she is truly feeling and hearing someone in a very similar position to her can help her to unpack those emotions. When something as complex as an eating disorder is present, it can be hard to differentiate between its feelings and your own. When you are constantly being gaslit and manipulated by a voice in your head, it can be hard to keep hold on your emotions and how your feelings truly feel. The Bulimic internal voice will hyper focus on anything that promotes the disordered behaviors and beliefs and try to overrule or dismiss anything else. Hearing this internal struggle from someone else's perspective can help young teens to feel validated and to secure their own feelings.

It also puts her in the position to offer support and guidance to others at the session, which can only be a good thing. If she feels she is helping others to make positive changes in their life this is bound to improve her self-worth and self-esteem. Not only that, but if she can make a positive difference to somebody else's recovery, this has to show her that on some level she can do the same within herself. Being part of a group focused on positive growth has to be a big bonus for her emotional well-being as well as her recovery.

5

DONT'S

*W*hat are the real no no's when dealing with Bulimia in your teenage daughter?

Having a teen with Bulimia can feel like having to walk on eggshells a bit as a parent. While you are having to relearn and change some of the ways you talk about food and eating, remember what she is going through. Everything you are doing is to help your sick child, if she had had an accident and broke her leg, you would adjust her life accordingly until she had made a full recovery. The same parental care and tenderness is required in this situation. There are some less obvious points and scenarios to directly avoid though.

Drawing attention to your daughter's eating habits in a negative way. Generally commenting on this frequently is also a significant issue. Both are going to be seriously damaging for your daughter to hear. You may feel like you're helping, but being overly critical and obviously observant are both going to put a dent not only in your daughter's confidence but in her willingness to talk to you. There are some simple ways to get around this though. Being more self-aware and rewording some of the phrases you use can go a long way. It is important to help your daughter release her habits, but not to draw attention to them all the time. There is a time and a place for trying to help your daughter and her views and high-pressure food related situations are typically not the time.

Some statements to watch out for could be;

- "Did you not eat today?"

This may feel like a very typical parent thing to say but break this statement down and read the root meanings of what you are actually saying. By saying this you're suggesting that you're shocked, unhappy or disappointed that she hasn't eaten today. Which will in turn make her feel guilty for worrying you or as if she has done something obviously wrong. This also belittled her eating disorder and her difficult feelings around food as this statement makes eating sound so simple. You may not have meant it this way, you may have even meant it in a caring way and to say that you're concerned about them, but this is not necessarily the way it will be received by someone struggling with Bulimia.

- "Be careful you don't choke!"

Any jokes or comments about how fast your daughter is eating are detrimental to her self-esteem and ability to feel safe in her own home. School and other more public places to eat may already feel like unsafe places, ensuring that her home feels like a safe place is critical. Your daughter may eat very fast and may eat large portions at one sitting, this is normal for someone struggling with Bulimia and should not be a point of ridicule.

While you may find it difficult to eat at that speed or volume, you're not struggling with a crippling eating disorder as a child, so your comment is unnecessarily hurtful. Again, if your daughter had broken her leg, would you complain at her for how slow she was walking on it? No, you would help her and make allowances for her new speed while she healed herself. Mental health IS physical health, your mind is and always has been part of your body. It is the driving seat for our bodies! Yet we dismiss and diminish mental health conditions simply because we cannot see the bruises and the marks left on our minds. Altering your mindset and approach towards your daughter's eating disorder is a non-excusable step, your daughter is a very sick teenager and not someone who should be a point of verbal abuse.

- "You will eat the rest of your food, that plate isn't going anywhere!"

Some parents feel the "tough love" approach is a good one to take. With a teenager that is so set in their thinking and will not budge, some parents come to the conclusion that the best option is to push their daughter back into 'normal' habits. This absolutely will not work and is a very poor choice on the part of her parents. This approach comes from a place of pure frustration on the part of the parent and you're putting that frustration outward onto an already fragile daughter. This statement essentially says, "I don't care how you feel, you will do as I tell you regardless!". It completely dismisses her feelings and prioritizes the needs of yourself, forcing her into a seemingly impassable situation. She either learns to force herself blindly into uncomfortable situations to please you or that she cannot eat around you at all and will simply isolate further. Either one of these scenarios is incredibly dangerous for the teenage girl suffering with Bulimia and harmful for your relationship as a whole. You are part of your daughter's core support system, if she doesn't have you then who does she have? Severing your relationship with your daughter is not an easily undone thing. She's also on the peak of adulthood and if she chooses to limit your relationship, it becomes much easier to make that happen in a more drastic way in the next few years.

What we say to our children really matters, there may be days you speak out of turn when the world is on your back but only you can then correct that behavior. We are our children's examples to the world, in later life they will use us as a measurement for what they should expect from potential future friends and partners. You could apologize, explain your having a tough time at work or wherever and tell her she has eaten more than enough already and you're proud of her. Just level with her and talk to her like another person, your human too and although snapping isn't ever a good thing or something you should make a habit of, when it does happen you have the power to use it as an opportunity to learn what not to do and how to handle it when you make mistakes. You also have to be prepared for her feelings to be hurt and for her to want to talk about that.

Being apologetic and showing her that your comment was uncalled for and is unjustifiable will help make sure she knows her feelings are valid. She has every right to be upset by your comment and it will most likely have triggered her eating disorder so be prepared for that. Alerting her therapist or support group could be helpful so that they can bring it up at their next session and help to provide support and another listening ear. It may feel minimal to you, but remember that she is already finding navigating her relationship with food intensely challenging, let alone adding extra tricky incidents in. With shame levels already dangerously high, ridicule from an outside source is unfortunately especially damaging.

If you made efforts to rectify the situation and this was a one off for you don't beat yourself up too much. Parenting is a hard and winding road and there is no manual. Sometimes it feels like you've fallen off the road and are rambling around somewhere down a dusty unrecognizable track, this is just the joys of parenthood. The one job on the planet with an ever-changing job description, each with a new breadth of tasks to complete and needs to meet. There are going to be times and probably have been before where you get things wrong or speak out of turn so don't panic too much. You did the right thing and did all you could to make amends, explain yourself and let her know that you made a bad choice, there isn't anything more that you could have done in this situation. Being reasonable and apologetic are really invaluable and go a long way in helping your child feel understood and simultaneously teaching her how to handle a situation that she spoke out of turn in. However, if you talk to your daughter like this often or have made comments similar to the above several times, you may want to seriously think about revising your approach to this situation. The one wonderful thing about being human is that for most things, we have complete control over our decisions and subsequently the choices that we make. This means that from one day to the next we can completely change our methods or approach to something, we are free to chop and change as we please. This power comes with responsibility though, as changing too frequently results in children raised in inconsistency. Take this opportunity now to re-think your approaches and set in place a plan to move forward. You could also let your daughter know that you've seen where you've been going wrong and that you're planning on making some positive change. Showing her that you're going to take a more emotionally mature approach to things and that you've spoken to her about it like an adult will validate any feelings she's been having and hopefully make her more positive about the future.

You plain and simply can't force your daughter through an eating disorder, no matter what you do or say. Even if she appears to have stopped her habits, she has most likely just got much better at hiding them or will pick them back up again soon after. The habits are not the beginning or the end of the problem when it comes to Bulimia, the relentless bulimic internal dialogue is where the real issues lie for sufferers. This needs careful work to be carefully unpicked; it will not be forced out by being told to leave. It will learn to adapt your daughter to guard her eating disorder related behaviors so they are done away from you. Unless you are with your daughter twenty-four-seven you can never be completely sure that the habits have stopped. For example, if she has been purging at home after school, she might instead adapt her habit so that she stops at a public toilet on the way home or purges in the toilets at school. Her self-hate will become monumentous if she is forced to stop her coping mechanisms. The internal voice will turn inwards and for an already isolated girl, self-harm and suicide become real risk factors. Eating disorders have the highest fatality rate of any mental disorder. Eating disorder patients are on average between 1.5 and 14 times more likely than peers their age to die. Two thirds of non-natural deaths (suicide) for eating disorders were tragically by those with Bulimia and Binge eating disorders.

Between 15% and 23% of those with bulimia nervosa report to have current suicidal ideation. (Lauren Mulheim PSyP CEDS, 2021) With suicide as a high-risk factor for your teenager anyway, risking pushing her away and making her feel alone is a very dangerous step to take, that could end up being detrimental. Is it not better to have a daughter on a slow and steady road to recovery than to risk not having a daughter at all?

Avoiding the topic of food is generally a better rule of thumb to go by and if and when the topic arises tread carefully. You're trying to help your daughter make progress does not get fixed overnight. Recovery and change are not set on an upward trajectory. It is completely normal and totally acceptable for your daughter to slip back sometimes and if anything, should be expected.

EATING IS CONTROL

Studies show that a large number of women with eating disorders shared the belief that much of their life was external to their control. A feeling of powerlessness against the stresses and pressure of life means that many have found comfort in the perceived control they can have over their food, eating habits or weight. Actually losing the weight in order to change their appearance was only really the first stepping stone for the sufferer. That motive has long since expired whether they are aware of it or not. It was initially thought that this belief system only aligned with sufferers of anorexia, but more recent studies suggest that there is virtually no difference in disorders like Bulimia Nervosa and the same harmful ideology is present. This makes understanding the powerful part that control plays in eating disorders a fundamental part of recovery for both parents, professionals and your daughter. The realities of Bulimia are much more complex than a desire to lose weight or change their appearance. Understanding that fact is a vital step for a parent to make in order to fully appreciate and understand their daughter's relationship with food and her body.

As a child, with little control over so much of her life this feeling is significantly amplified. For your daughter, managing her eating or weight so closely is a form of taking back some control in her life. By purging, binging, fasting etc., your daughter is escaping other negative emotions, thus she believes that she needs to continue on the disordered path that she is on or she will succumb to being inescapably unhappy. Most sufferers of an eating disorder describe an "out of control" feeling with food and they think that if they don't manage their relationship with food to minute levels that it will spiral out of control. She is also most likely seeking to escape the emotions she feels when bullies comment on her weight, or maybe it's the sinking feeling she gets when she sees thinner girls getting changed for PE at school. The scenario will vary and be individual for your daughter but that mass of negative feelings is very similar for a lot of sufferers.

The eating disorder then breaks this feeling down to immeasurable levels. In an attempt to problem solve and identify the source of this pain the mind goes on a rather peculiar detour. The next time she eats a full meal she might get the same emotions wash over her as well as guilt and shame. Her mind and body will begin to associate eating as the cause for all of her negative feelings about self and seeks to create actions to bring about change and escape those emotions. Instead of fixing the way she feels about herself her mind seeks to prevent her from experiencing the pain of intense self-hate and self-criticism. A short-term fix for a long term issue. This is the reason why she is so terrified to deviate from and leave her disordered actions in the past. Imagine all of that feeling coming flooding back all at once?

For any adult that is a feat to endure, let alone an adolescent girl. If this is forced or done without the correct support in place, she will be left to try and handle an overwhelming tidal wave of self-hate and negative feeling alone. You may be thinking "we all feel insecure sometimes", we absolutely do, but this is not the same feeling that your daughter has. Your teen is not just experiencing low esteem and insecurity but consuming and unsurpassable self-hatred. Your daughter does not think she deserves love or attention because of the way she looks. She feels substandard to her peers and the rest of the world by a long stretch, you're not dealing with regular anxiety but something much more severe and profound. Belittling this will only escalate the problem and make her feel more alone with her bulimic thoughts.

Try to think back to being a child. It might be hard to remember the feelings of being so out of control in your life when responsibility is so rife now. For teenagers they have just recently made the leap from one school into the next— or are about to—and exams and leaving school are ever looming. All of the above is all out of their control. They have very little say really in the way that their life will go for at least the next five years. They've just gone through a massive life change, leaving behind well-loved friends and familiar surroundings to be thrown into a high-pressure environment, it's no wonder why they feel the lack of control in their lives. Not to mention that the entire social hierarchy in school is decided by the people around you and one incident or accident can leave you tarnished with an unshakable and unsavory nickname. Your appearance immediately places you in a category and even if you drastically change it, you may never be allowed to live down the way that you used to look. For girls, if you aren't flawlessly beautiful, dashed with perfect make-up or have the trendiest bags and clothes, you're demoted as being ugly or not cool enough for boys' attention. The girls don't like you and won't entertain talking to you because of your low social status and the boys fear ridicule from their friends for the same reasons. Something we take so regularly for granted as an adult is something that they are yet to even experience. Having the freedom to shape yourself and to allow who you want around you, is a massive aspect of control that our teens lack.

The feeling of losing that minimal amount of control that you have over your life, could partly explain why the idea of letting go of not only their disordered behaviors but also re-thinking their protective mentality is such a monumental challenge for our teens. When you begin to think of food as an opportunity to gain emotional control, you will begin to understand that your daughter's complicated relationship with food is a very emotional one. Understanding and appreciating the realities of this will give you the best chance of being able to support her throughout her recovery. (Baxter Ekern, 9 April 2019)

This is so much more than a fear of gaining weight or fear of eating too much, food is woven into how your daughter measures her worth. Subsequently strong core emotional reactions are tied to certain scenarios that invisibly deplete her worth. Bulimia has much more depth than people imagined, or perhaps they would rather believe that their daughters' problems are far simpler. Either way, educating yourself on the ins and outs of Bulimia and similar disorders can only be a positive thing. Discovering the dark truths may be hard to hear, even more so when it is your child as the sufferer but knowing them could be the difference between giving your daughter bad and good support. These are the truths and realities that your daughter faces every day, imagine trying to unpick this as a teen. Denial can seem the more obvious option than confronting a truth such as this, it may seem so unrealistic and alien to her that these underlying issues are why she feels the way she does. Who can blame her? She will be simplifying her actions constantly and most likely not keeping a long-term track of how she is doing. Many go well into their adult lives before realizing they have serious self-esteem issues such as this, let alone seeking any kind of support for it. For a child to realize this alone is nothing short of a monumental breakthrough and utmost praise should be awarded. For someone in such a critical situation, a knowledgeable parent that is able to provide well allocated support very well could be the difference between life or death or remaining at home rather than being pushed into inpatient care.

6

DO'S

*A*s control is such a core part of Bulimia Nervosa one way of helping your daughter will be to give her some healthy ways of getting in the driver's seat with her food. The world of food is a vast and diverse world of undiscovered colors, tastes and textures to be explored and played with. Giving your daughter the opportunity to make choices, comparisons and have ideas about meals and meal ideas will help to divert her need for control with food into a healthier and much safer place. Cooking can be an exciting and interesting hobby, combining both a wealth of knowledge and hours of practical fun to be had. This is a brilliant way to put her need for control with food in a safer setting. Eating and food doesn't have to be a scary task forever and can be really enjoyable. Getting your daughter involved in meal prep and meal planning is a good way of getting started. Ask her opinions on flavors and textures, find out what her favorite kinds of foods are and what tastes she enjoys the most. If she loves to eat Italian food why not try making an Italian classic like lasagna, carbonara or pizza together. Getting her involved in meal prep with you is a good way of re-focusing and getting her to look past the fears of food and see the enjoyment and creativity behind making it. Play around with tastes and flavors and get your teens opinions on things. Value that opinion and follow her thoughts on ideas for food. If the worst happens, you end up with a weird tasting lasagna, you reassure her and give it another go. Allowing her some control and some freedom with her food will help to rekindle the love for food that your daughter once had or awaken a new one.

If you pack your daughter's lunches for school, why not try letting her pack them with you? This gives her healthy, positive control back to her relationship with food, in a safe space and with a member of her support system present. Try not to remain fairly neutral with comments, avoiding comments on portion sizes or what she has chosen to eat. This is her time to make decisions about her food, she's probably already feeling under a little pressure just on that basis so comments will naturally hit that bit harder when she is already extra sensitive. Even if she makes poor choices for her lunch, it's only 1 meal out of 3 in a day. Sometimes we just aren't that hungry either or don't fancy what's in the house, she's still a person underneath her Bulimia so try not to panic if the portion size dips or grows one day. Sustained periods of small portions however would be a concern that you could voice to her in a gentle and respectful way. Perhaps suggest adding an additional light and healthy snack, keep the requests small and low pressure. Something like a granola bar, piece of fruit or a light fruit muffin are all good options. If you're still worried and her portions remain unchanged then voice your concerns with her doctor or therapist.

Let her come shopping with you and pick out things she'd like to give a try. Grocery shopping is one more great way of being able to explore food safely for your teenager whilst also being supported through the process. Giving them the control aspect of picking their own ingredients that they'd like to try and the chance to do that whilst having your support is invaluable. Every small step is a big step for your daughter, so if she successfully picks out even 1 or 2 new things to try each shopping trip, then she's doing amazingly. She may struggle though, so be prepared for her to find the task of picking food out tricky. Patience is key, focus on getting your weekly shop and the house stocked up just as you normally would while she takes her time to look around. Your daughter may just shadow you for the first few shops, and eventually pluck up the courage to pick out something in a couple weeks' time. Every individual with Bulimia is different, there is no set course of action that can bring about an exact type of change. Try to go with the flow as best as you can. You've given your daughter a brilliant opportunity by bringing her along with you, the fact that she has tagged along is a big step in itself so try not to be downhearted if her progress is slow to begin with. She has the chance to make pressure free progress and that is a good place for her to start re-building safer habits and thought processes. Time is a great healer and so long as you're giving your daughter safe opportunities like this to explore healthier eating habits then you're doing everything you can.

This is also a really good opportunity for you both to get out of the house together, bond and chat. Maintaining a good relationship with your child while she struggles with an eating disorder is so vital for her recovery and ultimately her safety, as well as your own mental health. Sometimes parent's struggle to know how to communicate with their children when they suspect or know that something as serious is occurring. She's still the same little girl that used to decorate your house with crayon drawings and that begged for your cuddles, she's still a human beneath her Bulimia. Taking food off the table for a little while and chatting about non-eating related stuff will give her a little bit of time to break away from her problems and remind her that there is more to her life and your relationship than Bulimia. Eating disorders are consuming. Invading and contorting your world, it can begin to be tricky to remember a life or a world without your eating disorder for the sufferer. Some level of escapism is a useful tool for maintaining your daughter's mental health through recovery as well as your mental health as a parent. Talking about her social life, learning her friends' names and knowing her interests is all still part of being a parent too. This will help to remind her she has a life outside of her eating disorder and to cling onto that identity too. As well as being someone who suffers with Bulimia she is also still an individual with core beliefs, hobbies and a unique personality. Much of her self-worth and self-esteem rests on her exterior perception of her appearance, so re-focusing that and showing her some of your good qualities through discussion is bound to help. Simply showing her she is an interesting, intelligent and nice person to be around will hopefully help to realign her sense of self-worth and realize that liking yourself first begins with the person underneath the skin and bones. Talking and giving someone your time are both really underrated gifts that you can give to somebody. Doing things with her and prioritizing her a little will help her self-esteem immensely.

Charging head on at your family's problems twenty-four-seven is draining and it will begin to wear you down if you don't remember to engage in self-care or escapism activities. Anything from going for a walk alone or taking the time out of your week to meet up with a friend can all be ways of doing something for you. If your time is more limited, something as small as a relaxing bath or early night once a week can give you just that bit more time to relax. Adult life is non-stop and oftentimes incredibly stressful, we all need a little time for ourselves every now and again. Even though you are not the one diagnosed, an eating disorder is still a massive thing for a parent or a family to tackle. You're not a machine and you're not built to work like one, running yourself into the ground is not productive for you or your daughter. You can't be the best support system you can be, or even the best parent if you have pushed yourself over your limits. Use this as an opportunity for your daughter to show her that taking care of yourself is just as important as taking care of others. If you believe that your finding dealing with your daughter's eating disorder too challenging and your own mental and physical health is suffering, the best thing for all involved is for you to reach out for your own form of support too.

This could look like a therapist or counselor with knowledge of Eating disorders, but talking to your doctor first is the best course of action as they will be able to guide you safely, with a wealth of medical knowledge at hand. Daunting as it may be, this is not a reflection on you or a measure of your ability to parent that you are needing to reach out for support, but the opposite. You are making the sensible and ultimately best decision for you and your daughter and choosing to face your own issues too rather than running from them or burying them. So many parents bury their emotions and don't reach out for help where they need it.

Unfortunately, our society carries this belief that we must run ourselves into the ground for our children or we are not a good parent. Sacrifice is obviously a fundamental part of parenthood, but this does not apply as a baseline rule to all scenarios. Your children need you, so if you push yourself into the realms of self-destruction you aren't going to be able to be there for them. Part of being a responsible parent is also maintaining your own health, both physical and mental, so that you are able to be the best parent you can be. The philosophy that our wellness doesn't matter as a parent is not feasible. This does not mean prioritizing your needs over the happiness or health of your child though and is not an excuse to be derogatory or demeaning towards them. Part of being a good parent is not blaming your children for your emotions. You are an adult and it's up to you to manage your emotions, not your kids and certainly not your teenage daughter struggling with an eating disorder. This situation is no doubt hard on you, but it's up to you what you do with those negative emotions and whether you channel that into healthy coping mechanisms or unhealthy, toxic ones.

As a result of the above theory so many parents sacrifice their own happiness and suppress their emotions. Their relationship with their children often suffers drastically as both become caught in the crossfire. Your daughter will most probably remember this time in her life for the remainder of it, so how you reacted and how you chose to conduct yourself as a parent will stay with her. That can either be in a traumatic way if you choose to let your emotions rule you or it can be for the relentless way that you supported her. Our parents are our role models for life too, so she will call upon this time when she is in similarly difficult situations with her own children for advice and silent wisdom. Set an example not only for your possible future grandchildren but for the woman that your daughter will become and help give her a shining example of how human kindness can work. Our children are going to meet a lot of bad people in their lives that will look a lot like good people, the only way to distinguish between the two is by having a crystal-clear image of what you should expect from others. This is what makes getting support for yourself so important, so that you can show her what the sensible course of action is in a situation where your mental health or wellness is compromised. We are not machines and we aren't built to run twenty-four-seven. Even machine's need new parts and have to be serviced every now and again, they need maintenance and care—nothing is indestructible on this earth. Give your mind the healthy maintenance it needs so that it can begin to run at full capacity once again.

Seeking Non-Medical Support

Another way of aiding your daughter's recovery is gathering support for her outside of the doctors and therapist's office. Letting her immediate family know a little about what things to watch out for can help make her inner world that bit simpler. More often than not we accidentally say things and we're unaware of how seriously that can be taken and inter-preted by somebody else and most will gladly alter their words when given more information. In eating disorders in general, there are a lot of situations or topics of conversation that need to be handled with care and awareness. Mealtimes or any social event where food is present is a definite one to remain slightly more self-aware at. Encourage your family members or close family friends to do the same.

You don't need to dive into your daughter's personal experi-ences or personal details if she would rather you didn't, but giving them a rough idea of how she is feeling and under-lining some obvious no's no's to them will help both your family and friends. As a result your teenager too. If your daughter is happy for you to disclose some more personal details surrounding her experiences with Bulimia then do so.

The more aware that your family is of her situation, the better they will be able to handle scenarios with fragility and kindness. Eating disorders are largely misunderstood and a large portion of the population is unaware of the in's and out's. There are also a lot of stigmas that come with having an eating disorder, particularly in older generations who grew up at a time when Bulimia and similar disorders were rarely recognized and there was little treatment available.

Society was also a very different place back then, almost unrecognizable to the one we know today. In the last 50 years we've gone from being taught that you must hide your true self, your problems and struggles from the outside world entirely to being encouraged to speak out about personal problems. Fear of being shunned, shame and pride kept so many from reaching out for support or discussing their problems outside of their homes. Now we live in a society that encourages and congratulates individuals to speak out, the new focus on awareness and education. You may run into some negative comments or perceptions, so be prepared for that. Some people will be willing to listen and be open to hear the realities and facts surrounding Bulimia but sadly, this might not be the case for everyone. If anyone is being continually negative and unhelpful, you may want to seriously think about how much of a good idea it is to have them around your daughter and subsequently in your life. Eating disorders are understandably an uncomfortable topic for some, but when you're trying to create a positive and inclusive environment for your daughter, this mindset can be extremely harmful and hindering. Speaking about your daughter's issues will likely determine who should be attending social events when she is present. Use your judgment and don't be scared to lose some people, sadly not everyone is optimistic and open minded but that is their problem; certainly not yours or your teenagers.

For example, you could say that she's struggling a little with self-esteem and eating as a whole, so, to avoid any comments that draw attention to her and food or her appearance. Talking a little about triggers and the serious implications that they have for her mental health is another good step. Trigger or triggered is becoming a colloquially used term, but unfortunately with an incorrect definition. Teenagers are now using 'triggered' in a humorous way to infer that something has upset them or is inconvenient to them. For example, "I went shopping with Sadie on Saturday and I was triggered because there was a woman wearing an entire bright pink outfit". To many of us this statement sounds utterly ridiculous but it's sadly a common thing amongst young people now. It may seem harmless and at worst a silly or stupid thing to say, but it does have more serious implications. It completely downplays the severity behind the true definition of a trigger and so many people who suffer with triggers as a reality of mental health issues feel ridiculed. As a result, many grow up with an incorrect, oversimplified and disrespectful view of what a trigger is and what it feels like to be triggered. Being triggered is also an individual thing, although there are a lot of similarities how it shows itself is largely dependent on the nature of the disorder and the issues surrounding that. A PTSD trigger would differ and vary from a Bulimia Nervosa trigger but there may also be some similarities. Describing exactly what your daughter's experience of being triggered is like is the best course of action to keep your family or friends best informed.

For closer family members you may want to go into more detail and give some more specifics, it depends totally on what your daughter is comfortable with. Maybe you are planning a family BBQ or having a family member or friend stay with you. Give the invited guests a little heads up before they get to yours, so that there are no awkward conversations in front of and around your daughter. You don't want to risk her thinking or feeling that you're discussing her or her Bulimia behind her back, this could push her further away from you and leave her feeling like she can't trust or confide in you.

With triggering comments or moments minimized in her surroundings, your daughter should hopefully begin to gain some more confidence surrounding food or at the very least avoid unnecessary obstacles. Recovery is a tough enough journey, so every little positive helps make that road just that bit easier to walk down.

You could also discover through talking openly about your daughter's issues, that one of your family friends or a relative has experienced an eating disorder or other serious self-esteem issues in the past. Gaining some insight from a fellow adult could be immensely useful for you as a parent. Providing this person is trustworthy, you could take the opportunity to talk a bit more openly about some of the questions you may have. It could be useful for your daughter to speak to someone that she knows who also understands how it feels to be directly in her shoes. If your relative or friend is an appropriate person to talk to your daughter and if your daughter is willing to, then the two of them chatting could be very beneficial for both involved. Your daughter could gain some experience from someone who has gone through the recovery process already and has struggled through the feelings that she is currently experiencing. They may also be able to share some useful tips and information and knowledge to help get her through certain uncomfortable situations or stages of recovery. Hindsight is a wonderful thing, someone who has already gone through the ups and downs of the recovery process will be able to give your daughter all the things that they wish they could have had at the time. This could prove invaluable to her mental health and her overall recovery. This person could be another positive voice that helps keep her focused and optimistic throughout.

CREATE A POSITIVE ENVIRONMENT AROUND FOOD

One strong action you can make is to start helping to create a healthy and happy atmosphere surrounding food for your daughter. Even on the day's she is at school she eats ⅔ meals at home. This could be through something as simple as having some of the family's favorite songs on or watching a classic movie while you all eat. Mealtimes are additionally a great time for family fun and bonding, so this is the perfect opportunity to have some fun with food! Getting the whole family involved in making a meal is a perfect way to bring some lightness to the table and just have some silly fun together as a family. Be careful to remain self-aware throughout whatever activity it is that you choose and make sure that you aren't focusing on any of the previously mentioned soft spots in earlier chapters. Try to keep the mood light and as much as the focus is on creating tasty food to share, it's also on enjoying the process. It can be tricky so know what sort of food related family fun is appropriate and what isn't appropriate for your teenager to experience without resulting in a trigger or outburst.

Below is some guidance and a few suggestive ideas on how your family can have fun, mindfully.

- Play relaxing music in the background.

This will help to create a relaxing atmosphere and give your teenager something else to think about other than her food. Even if the music is not the center of attention it will help to create a positive association with mealtimes and eating.

- Play musical games at the table. Use a Bluetooth speaker, apple tv etc. Have each person choose a song and discuss the reasons why.

This is a great way to bring humor to mealtimes whilst also giving everyone the chance to play some of their favorite music. It also opens up the chance for an at length discussion on some of the family's favorite music and their personal reasons why. This is also a fabulous way to divert the focus from food and onto an enjoyable and humorous topic.

- Cook together!

Cooking together as a family gives everyone the chance to get involved and enjoy working as a team to prepare a meal to share. Choose something challenging and fun to make and give everyone individual parts of the process. This is a great way to de-value food for your daughter. Being involved in the making process will hopefully divert some of her focus from the eating stage and onto the creation stage. Pizza making is a particularly good one, although you may want to adapt recipes and especially toppings to include healthy options too so your daughter has a selection and doesn't feel pressured into eating something she'd rather not eat.

- Barbecues

Although this one is largely weather dependent, if the sun is out seize the opportunity to enjoy eating special occasion food outside. Barbecues are the perfect chilled out eating setting. Most of the attention is normally on not burning food and the nice weather and thus your daughter won't feel the center of attention. It's also a chance to try new and exciting flavor combinations. The unique smoky flavor that goes along with barbecue is wonderful to experiment with and can be mixed with a whole range of sweet, sour and spicy flavors to create sticky and smoked heaven. If you are vegetarian or vegan there is no need to miss out, there is a wide variety of BBQ options for those to choose from. Smoked and stuffed peppers are a particularly popular simple dish that is incredibly tasty and customizable to suit your preferred tastes.

- Upgrade your mealtime set up

Switching up your cutlery and crockery will help to give mealtimes a new lease of life and a new look. You've most probably been holding onto your old plates and your table arrangement for the majority of your life as a parent, so why not use this as an opportunity to brighten up your dinner times. Making the table and your plates a more inviting place to eat at will help make the entire mealtime experience that bit easier. A more inviting table, the more likely you are to want to sit and eat at it. It will not fix all of your daughter's eating issues by any means, but it will at least make the space for her to eat in a more pleasant one.

- Switching up your dinner time location

Changing your ordinary dinner location to a new one can also help to create a more positive and refreshing environment. If your old faded table has been sitting in the corner of your kitchen for as long as you can remember, this could be the opportunity you've been looking for to move it to a new location in the house. Jazz it up with new tablecloth or some fairy lights, hanging baskets or a wall hanger besides. Make your eating area an interesting and inviting place to be and it will be a more pleasant place for your daughter to eat freely.

Although these things may seem trivial and otherwise insignificant, every little helps when it comes to battling something as mammoth as an eating disorder. Every little change is a step in the right direction. Our hands are tied as parents for so many things throughout our daughter's recovery process and feeling like a helpless bystander in your own daughter's life is incredibly challenging but unfortunately common. Making the most of every opportunity you get to help, however big or small, will keep both yours and your daughters mental health in a better place. Any action you may take to aid your daughter's recovery or make her life easier is a positive. Your teenager will need a strong and willing support system to help catch her when she falls and pick her up when she feels stronger. Knowing that you are present in her life and are trying to make positive change will be a large relief to her. So much of the worry behind an eating disorder is shame related and most often, we care more about what our parents think than anyone else. Letting your parents down or thinking that you've disappointed them can be a real heavy burden to drag through life with you, and not one that's easy to shake. Your helpful acts will help to mute that Bulimic voice in her head that assures her she is the worst daughter on the planet and in fact prove the opposite. She is a strong and capable young woman who can beat this disorder and kick it to the curb.

. . .

Freedom With Clothes

Your daughter may be slightly further down the line with her Bulimia and if this is the case, you may have noticed that she's started to lose weight. Her clothes may be starting to hang off her more and more but you're not sure how to bring attention to it without being insensitive, am I right? Baggy or loose-fitting clothes might also feel safer for her, as they hide her body and aren't tight on any sensitive areas. Clothes being tight fitting can trigger the feelings of being 'too big' as much as being teased at school by bullies. Shopping for some new, more comfortable clothes is another excellent way for your teen to get some control back with her body, and get creative with a new style. Although it is a topic that should be broached tentatively. You could try suggesting a shopping trip for the whole family or go one on one with her as a Mother-Daughter, Father-Daughter shopping trip or by saying you need some new clothes and wondered if she would like to go as well. Give her freedom to choose when she gets to the shops and respect her choices and opinions, the key of this trip is not really getting new clothes but getting her comfortable and putting her in a position of control, as well as hopefully having some fun! This means being gentle with your opinion and taking a back seat on choices, no matter what she chooses. Picking a few items out for yourself will take some of the pressure off her too and give you guys something to chat about- as well as getting you an ungraded wardrobe!

Avoid any comments about her body or pushing her into wearing something she doesn't want to, this is about her making choices about clothes. Even if you feel that you're being helpful, sometimes saying less is more, simply being with her and offering neutral opinions or encouragement when she needs it is a strong positive for your daughter.

Even if she is only confident enough to pick out 1 or 2 items this time, that's still a really good step for her to have taken and you should both be proud of her!

Online shopping may be an alternative if your daughter is uncomfortable with shopping around other shoppers. Many moms out there have been looking for new sized jeans post baby and have looked across at the thinner, younger girl standing at the pile of their old size and felt that twinge of self-consciousness and can relate to the way your daughter will feel seeing other more idealistic bodies. Online shopping sites have boomed through the Covid-19 pandemic and there are now more online sites with fast delivery services than ever. Online shopping has become so much easier than it was pre-2020, with many sites offering payment via apple pay and delivering further afield for less. Sitting with her while she browses or just giving her some cash to have some freedom with are both good ways of going about the online alternative. This could be slightly problematic as you're possibly dealing with clothes being pictured on model's bodies. It might be worth you going through a few of the sites she likes before she looks at them with you and seeing if they use mannequins or models to show off their clothes. Ebay is normally a safer bet as many of their listings use images only including items of clothing and there are most likely more sites out there. Again this depends largely on your daughter and if looking at models is something that will trigger her eating disorder, she might want to refrain from shopping until you've managed to find some more appro-priate sites. You could also try going through sites for her and seeing if they use mannequins or models to show off their clothes. This is another way for you to be able to help and get actively involved in her recovery as well as having some all important 1 on 1 time with your teenager. You should also refrain from making too many judgmental comments about the fashion seen on your teens sites of choice, although it may be shocking to our generation that judgment is still not helpful for our children. Our generation had things that I'm sure our parents could have laid eggs at the sight of, that is just a part of living in our ever-changing society.

Spending the day digging through thrift stores or going to a flea market could be another alternative as these rarely have any kind of advertisement. Although it doesn't sound like the typical family fun day out, these are great places for finding cost effective hidden gemstones as well as killing some time together. You can find a wide variety of low-priced clothes as well as having a fun time looking through the wide variety that amasses at these stores and social events. Loosen up and have some silly fun together! Trying on clothes that you'd never dream of wearing out together and having a hard laugh about it will help remind your daughter that image doesn't have to be so serious. Appearances can be enjoyed, altered and played with without their being severe consequences. So much of the belief system behind eating disorders is so hard to erase as the alternative feels so detrimental. Using humor is a great, low-pressure way to help your daughter to realize this. Take the lead on this and just have fun! If you're not the most confident person yourself then this could be an opportunity to push yourself out of your comfort zone a little too, what better reason than to help your child get back some of her comfort and confidence with clothes. If she's not comfortable being this free with her clothes and body yet then don't worry, just try to enjoy the time you have together and use it to grab some awesome bargains while you're there!

Clothes may be a sensitive topic as a whole, so if your daughter doesn't feel up to shopping then that's ok. Looking for clothes confronts your body image issues head on and trying to deliberate the correct size can be intensely scary for sufferers of Bulimia. Creativity and freedom are only part of shopping for clothes, the darker side forces you to think more closely about your body in order to make choices, for a Bulimic, this is a massive ask. Confronting something about yourself that you have huge insecurities around is a mammoth task and not one that should be rushed, it's important that your daughter remains in control of all aspects of her recovery. There is no set speed with how fast she'll make progress and every individual sufferer of Bulimia is different. She might have reached the point that she's stopped some of her harmful habits but still feels uncomfortable looking at and even trying on clothes, it just depends on what she personally finds more challenging or is comfortable with. Triggers are so varied and so is the intensity at which individual sufferers will experience them. For one person this could result in a slight setback that day with their eating or it could cause a catastrophic downward spiral, there is just no telling and neither experience is wrong or right. Try not to be discouraged and don't blame your daughter or make her feel guilty for not going. Prioritize the area's that she is progressing in, no matter how small and make sure to praise her. Making sure she knows that you're proud of her for every hard step forward she is taking. When you already feel that something is wrong with you, it makes progress feel mandatory and like your continually playing catch up with normality. Letting her know that you see all the effort she's putting in and giving her some hard-earned credit for that should help to remind her that her differences from others and her struggles with food make her progress even more exceptional. Also remind her that eating disorders are so much more common than she thinks, both in adults and teens, and that most people just don't talk openly about it. It's not that these issues don't exist for anybody else, but they are just not discussed openly or they are purposefully hidden. This is not because Bulimia or any of the other disorders are anything to be ashamed of, but is a sad recognition of the state that our society is in. Tough topics of conversation are regrettably not encouraged nearly as much as they should be and sadly so many teenagers share this strange belief that none of their peers have any issues of their own. We only learn that the opposite is true when we gain wisdom through age and experience. As an adult, we realize that our world is full of singular and vastly unique people, nearly all of them have some level of issues of their own. We're an emotional species and so throughout our life we pick up trauma and personal issues on some level.

You could also try explaining some of this to her. It may be hard for her to imagine as the world she inhabits at school is so image focused, but let her know that once you leave the world is very different to how school is. Yes, there are judgmental people everywhere, but the judgment from the majority of people is far less, most adults realize that we are all going through our own stuff. Within the walls of most homes are secrets that the outside world couldn't imagine, but just because you can't see something doesn't mean that it doesn't exist. Mental health problems are nothing to be ashamed of, the sad fact is the only reason people think that they are is through a massive lack of education and understanding. If talking were more normal, then we'd all know far more about the ins and outs of our minds and how regularly so many of us are affected.

. . .

Sarcasm

Sarcasm slips into the undefined category between well-meant humor and unhelpful comments; it can be tricky to identify where the line is when it comes to sarcastic humor or comments especially when a teenager with Bulimia is present. If you're typically a comical person who uses light-hearted sarcasm to humor your family and friends, it's understandable that you might be unsure on how to proceed around your daughter. The fact you've stopped to think about it is a really good step in the first place! The best way to go about this is to avoid making any sensitive or trigger-able topics of conversation into a sarcastic comment. Even if it's completely well intentioned or you're trying to break the awkwardness with some humor, it's near impossible to know what thing's will set off a response from your daughter's bulimia. With the risk factor so high it's best to just avoid any kind of jokes surrounding food, weight, appearance and eating disorders all together.

Any other topics of conversation however are totally fine, you just may want to remain more aware of your overall comments around her more sensitive stuff. We all have subjects we find tricky to discuss and there is no doubt some things you can't say to your partner, friends or parents, the same rule simply applies here. Lighthearted humor directed at other things should be ok though, for example if you're sitting round the dinner table and you crack a joke about something that happened that day at work, this would be a good way to utilize sarcasm to create a light atmosphere. So long as your work story was un-food, weight, appearance, or ED related you should be totally fine sharing it over dinner. You're still a 'normal' family and you can still crack jokes and be silly and humorous without it having a deeper meaning. Having a daughter with Bulimia doesn't mean completely redefining life, it just means making some alterations to some of the things we do. Developing a keen awareness of self and those around you is a great skill to have, not only when dealing with someone with an eating disorder but as a general rule of thumb through life. The more conscious you are of those around you the more in tune you are with how to tackle situations appropriately, which means less butting heads or accidentally hurting people in the long run.

Eating disorders are not jokes and once you have seen what they can do to a person it makes it incredibly hard to make it funny anymore. For the sufferer a joke will be dismissive and demeaning and cause unnecessary pain to a person who is already living with surreal weights on their back. Not all things are simple in life, this is a very complex issue that needs to be treated carefully for the person struggling with it to begin to recover.

7

FAMILY INVOLVEMENT

*M*aking your home and your family space a place of acceptance, safety and non-judgment is a difficult but achievable task. If you live in a home with multiple children, getting your daughter's siblings on board can be very challenging. Age is obviously a large factor and how much and how little you tell your children is largely age dependent. If your daughter's siblings are a little older, then getting them on the same page should be a bit easier but remember the news could still be a shock for them and eating disorders are complex and confusing enough for adult non-sufferers, let alone a child, or young teen. Make sure to speak clearly and be ready to give in detail descriptions and explanations. Answering their questions respectfully will also make sure they feel that they can talk openly to you about anything they are worried or curious about. It can be a scary thing having a sister in the clutches of Bulimia and raises a lot of questions in the minds of children. They are just seeking to understand at the end of the day, so don't take their questions (however many) to heart or let them frustrate you. This is uncharted territory for most children and teenagers, they may only know what they have seen on tv or heard about at school. We forget as adults that if we don't have much parental intervention to tell us the true meanings of things, as children we tend to make up a lot of our own rationale for things by absorbing what's around us. This is where not giving your children enough or the correct information becomes harmful and can lead to confusion and upset.

As a parent it is your duty to safely guide your children through life's experiences and definitions, helping to provide clarity, advice and support where they need it. If they feel unable to turn to you for answers to their questions they will go elsewhere. Social media and the internet as a whole are both notorious for putting out false or angled information, but this is where so many of our children now go looking for answers if we are not there to give them to them. Pages on TikTok, Instagram and snapchat are all loaded with false media but our children consume these apps regularly, most probably every day. Social media in itself is responsible for so many issues surrounding self-esteem, body confidence and eating disorders directly. It is a minefield for misinformation, both in the filtered and edited images we see and the phony information pages that can be written by anybody now. Although there has been a lot of growth in the presence of body positivity on social media in the last five years, there is still (and probably will always be) wildly incorrect information available online, for free. The majority of this information is broadcast through the previously mentioned apps that our teens use so frequently.

As these posts, sites or videos are shared throughout friend groups, classes and schools it is no wonder why so much false information is spread so rapidly. With a class, year group or even school full of children surrounding themselves with this information there is no wonder that it becomes so concreted into their minds. Making it even more critical that, as parents, we sit down and have the difficult or uncomfortable conversations with our kids and let them ask all the silly or embarrassing questions that they'd like to.

There are also sadly many people who feel that pretending to have an eating disorder on social media, in order to gain attention, is something they'd like to do. There will always be attention seekers in the world and those with no shame or empathy to the real sufferers, the rise of 'influencers' on social media has meant that now your issues can become trendy and that can pay a nice wage. With material motives, the content that they put out is purely focused on pay and getting people to hit that like, subscribe or share button. This obviously results in so much incorrect information being put out and sufferers of real disorders are left feeling ridiculed and deflated. Differentiating between genuine pages and those looking purely to gain views and followers is more difficult to navigate than ever. These online characters are essentially actors that play a role, and some play that role very convincingly.

For younger children, wordage and clear information is everything. Make sure your explanations are truthful and make sense, this avoids any awkward situations for them if they are discussing their sister's disorder at school or nursery. They might not fully understand a teacher's raised eyebrows or shocked look, but they will know that something wasn't right about the interaction and will most likely wonder what it was. Broad statements that offer little information may temporarily defuse any questions and wriggle you out of an uncomfortable conversation but can result in confusion and potentially awkward or traumatizing situations for the young child in the future. For example; if you tell them that your daughter just has a tummy bug but they then later see her making herself sick, this would result in possible confusion and even trauma for that child. As previously discussed, trauma is largely dependent on perspective so although this may seem like a trivial event to you; this could be a very prevalent and harmful memory for your child in future years to come.

While many would encourage parents to leave younger children completely out of the situation for fear of potential trauma, it is a great challenge that any two or more people that live in a home together cannot discover another's regular habits. Especially as your daughter will most likely have obvious behavioral changes, such as mood swings or staying in her room or the bathroom for longer periods of time. Children are very intuitive and aware of their surroundings, so they will no doubt pick up on this and start to form their own narrative for why things are happening. Obviously, over sharing and giving out age-inappropriate information is just as damaging, but there is a safe middle ground. You can try rephrasing or simplifying statements to make them more user friendly, as well as adding an approachable and calm tone to match. For example;

Six-year-old "Mommy why is she not eating much anymore at dinner time and being sick sometimes, is she sick?"

Parent: "She is sick, she has something called an eating disorder. That's basically a fancy way of saying that she is finding food tricky and feeling a bit under the weather too!"

Six-year-old: "oh no, that's sad. Will she get better?"

Parent: "Of course! She just needs some love and in time she will get better on her own. I took her to see the doctor and he is going to help too."

There is no perfect conversation to have about these tough things in life, so keep that in mind. Even if you feel you could have done better at explaining, there is always a next time to try to reconnect with your child on the subject. It might take a few conversations before your child gets a proper understanding of the situation, so don't be disheartened if they come back to you again with more queries, theories or suggestions. You bringing it up again will also show that you're comfortable talking about this topic with them and let them know that it's okay to do the same. The fact that one of you has made the effort to start a conversation is a strong and positive step for you and your little or big one.

With difficult situations like this, many children also choose to remain completely silent about the issue as they feel too awkward or uncomfortable raising such a potentially sensitive topic alone. They will most likely fear your reaction too, as emotions are already running high in such a fragile scenario. You may want to start the conversation first with your children to bring them up to speed on what is happening and reduce any anxiety they are having about bringing it up naturally. They might be worried that they've got the wrong end of the stick or don't want to risk upsetting you by talking about it, even if they are harboring worries about their sister. Children tend to internalize and absorb a great deal without even really knowing, it's what makes them able to learn and retain so much knowledge.

I'm sure we have all wished at one or more points in our adult life to have that youthful ability to capture and retain knowledge that we utilized frequently and freely in our younger years. In childhood your brain is growing at an alarming rate and it does this through being so sponge-like in nature. While this is a great evolutionary tool to maximize child development, it also means that in harmful or traumatic environments our children take in a lot more than we would like to think. Mostly as a survival tool, as learning from our negative environments is still a natural part of human nature and something that we will have to do many times throughout our lifetime.

However, without much parental intervention or when regular trauma is present, our children may make drastic assumptions that can become knotted deeply into their core beliefs and will travel with them through to adulthood. This makes having conversations at tough times absolutely necessary and making the conversation a pleasant encounter for your child just as important.

Try to keep the atmosphere of the conversation relaxed and casual. You could start by saying something like "hey I've been meaning to have a chat with you about something" keeping your tone light and friendly. A good time to do this is when your attention is on something else and not focused directly on your child, as too much attention or pressure can put a lot of children off raising their true concerns or feelings. While driving, watching tv or washing the dishes are all good options where the mood is already relaxed and the main focus of your attention is diverted. Be open to the fact that they may have already formed ideas in their heads and will want to ask you about those. They may be incorrect or seem silly to you but don't ridicule or make your child feel stupid. Appreciate that is the way it has seemed for them, you're an adult and have facts and knowledge that they don't. They are only capable of thinking what a child is thinking. Take the time to correct them gently and explain at length, using simple words and examples or comparisons if you can. As earlier mentioned though, there isn't a one size fits all conversion to have with your child, so long as you're understanding and informative with them you're doing brilliantly.

Making your daughters siblings, school, responsible adults and teachers aware of the goings on at home will also help to give your child another place to go for support. Letting them also know what you have told your child and how much they know and don't know will help them to be able to support them in line with the support they are receiving at school. They'll also be able to answer any questions your child asks about eating disorders at school honestly but in a way that you're comfortable with. Having them as another pair of eyes and ears at school is also a good tool for you as a parent. They'll be able to keep a look out for any worrying signs of behavior changes or topics of conversation with peers. If they spot any changes in your child's behavior, attitude or academic performance they will be able to flag it up with you and approach the topic with the child from a more empathetic angle. Keeping your child's school in the dark could result in misunderstandings and missed signs of decline in your child, thus bringing more stress to their world. Worry and stress can both be problematic in siblings of someone with an eating disorder, as they struggle to grapple with the powerlessness that you also feel as a parent. Children also associate things like eating disorders as being very serious and they may be worried that their sister may never get better at all. It's difficult for them to grapple with the idea that the person that they have grown up with, the person that they laugh and are silly with, is also harboring a serious mental health condition. These two identities are understandingly challenging for children to align into one single person.

Schools also have policies and a duty of care code to adhere to. If they see worrying signs in your child, then it is their job to take some kind of action on behalf of the wellness of the child. This could be discussing it with a parent, a higher member of staff or putting some kind of special measure in place to make learning and the school environment an easier place to learn and play. If the teacher is already aware of Bulimia being present in a sibling in the child's home, this should help them to skip a step and get the right support in place sooner. A large amount of schools now have school counselors either on site or that visits regularly, it may be that your child just needs another safe figure to talk to about their feelings and concerns. Having a positive, safety net outside of your home can be massively beneficial, sometimes hearing someone with an outside perspective tell you that things will be ok is just different to hearing the same thing from a loved one. It also means they have someone angled directly at discussing and valuing their feelings. Where you are normally stretched between all of your children and trying to ensure that they all feel appreciated, respected and heard, this individual would be able to zone in more person-ally on your individual child's feelings. This can only be a positive for you and your family.

Don't feel that your child needing outside support is a poor reflection on your ability as a parent, it is simply them strug-gling a little and nothing deeper than that. We all struggle sometimes, no matter how much support we have available. Life just gets on top of us all sometimes and it is nobody's fault. What's important is that your child's change in behavior has been noted and there is now a solution actively in place to give them the little bit of help that they need.

ONE DAY AT A TIME

Recovery is a long and difficult process for any individual, bumps along the way are to be expected. Take every day as it comes, you can't be expecting your daughter to get into therapy and magically do a 180 with her belief system and her habits. Take every meal one at a time and see how she does. Small steps forward are still strong steps forward no matter the size and any progress she makes is helping to get her a bit further down the road to recovery. Taking her recovery one step, day or meal at a time will help maintain a positive environment for your daughter to eat around. If you're continually thinking back and measuring her progress and stretching out a plan of hopeful milestone points for the future then you are going to be adding a large amount of pressure to your daughter's plate, as well as your own. You are not the one in the driving seat of your daughter's disorder and no matter how much you do in this situation, it is not up to you how this pans out or how fast she progresses and recedes. You can help her greatly, but ultimately this situation is very much out of your control. See every mealtime as an opportunity to help your daughter and if any progress is made, be proud of her for that. This means making her as comfortable, the environment as positive and relaxed as it can be and not passing unhelpful judgmental or overly observative comments throughout the meal.

A "make your own plate" kind of meal is a perfect option, especially if your daughter has chosen things to be put out in the spread and, maybe even helped you to prepare some of the dishes. Placing everything out on the table and giving everybody the freedom to have as much or as little as they want, without judgment or speculation is invaluable and beneficial for your daughter. If she is uncomfortable with serving at the table with everybody present, you could instead ask every family member to come into the kitchen one by one and fill their own plates individually. This way she has both the freedom to pick and choose her portion sizes and make individual decisions with her food without the pressure of a table of people watching.

Not having rushed schedules around food time is something else that can be hugely beneficial to your daughter. If your kids rush in from school, sit and eat and are then rushed out the door to go to a club or to the shops, this creates a pressurized atmosphere at mealtimes. Make food times a relaxing family time, mealtimes are a great opportunity to catch up with your children and chat about their days. Let's face it, finding time to sit down and really talk to your children is challenging when your navigating work, cleaning, cooking and pet care. Being an adult means running on an incredibly tight schedule and many of us are admittedly guilty of not finding time for as much quality time as we'd like with our families and children. Making mealtimes about quality time and not just feeding everybody as quickly as possible can give you an extra 30 mins or more per meal to spend diving deeper into the minds of your kids. Checking in with your children, however old, is vital and can help you to spot problems arising and get support in place where it's needed.

This will also help you to maintain that close bond that oftentimes gets lost with no sign of return through the teenage years of our children's life. As they naturally start seeking independence, so many parents think that independence is given by cutting off a large majority of their interactions and communication with their teen. Independence doesn't mean that we stop talking to our children, they are growing up but don't need to grow into a stranger. Keeping simple mealtime conversations going about their day; showing an interest and talking to them as an equal will all help to keep you and your teens relationship on a good level. Dinner time brings a purpose to sitting down with your chil-

dren. Rather than trying to sit them down for a chat specifi-
cally to catch up with how they are, talking to them at the
table offers a less pressured setting and gives them an alternative purpose to sit down- to enjoy good food together as a
family!

It may take some time for your teens, tweens or children to
warm up to the idea of dinnertime conversation but don't be
disheartened. Stick with it. Routines create habits and with
enough time you might find that your kids naturally become
more inclined to join in on the dinnertime conversation.
Letting them freely choose to contribute or not to will help
maintain a low-pressure vibe and let them know that you're
not trying to force them into anything. Some kids are just
quieter than others too, so if one of your children is chewing
your ear off while the other only says a few sentences, don't
panic. Being a quiet person isn't necessarily a negative char-
acteristic and is only really a sign of something sinister when
it occurs suddenly. If one day your child is the biggest chat-
terbox going and then suddenly, they're regularly quiet or
withdrawn you should absolutely take that as a sign that
something is a foot. Having catch ups with your kids at mealtimes as a regular thing will help to give you a baseline for
how they're each doing. This kind of relaxed but regular
conversation is another excellent way of taking the pressure
out of your daughter's mealtimes and giving her alternative
topics to think about and discuss.

YOUR DAUGHTER IS NOT A PROBLEM TO BE FIXED

Many parents jump into action mode when they find out
that their daughter is struggling with a mental health condition like Bulimia. In a well-meant attempt at trying to help

they start trying to 'fix' her typically by talking or taking action to try to make her progress down the road of recovery at an impossible pace. While this is typically meant in a kind and considerate way, it's not in actuality all that helpful and in fact can be a massive hindrance. Bulimia cannot be forced out or away from your child and there is no amount of pushing that is going to help that. Less is so much more with something as layered as Bulimia. The more that you push her to get better the more you are going to make her feel like there is something wrong with her, thus pushing her ever deeper into the depths of her self-hatred. Pressure is Bulimia's best friend and your daughter's worst enemy in this situation. Treating your daughter like she is something that needs to be corrected is really not going to help, it is not her having the eating disorder that is the problem it is what the eating disorder does to her. The issue is incredibly complex and is to do with the disorder itself, your daughter is virtually powerless to control the disorder so picking a fight with her about things isn't going to help at all. This is something that needs to be talked through in detail with a therapist or medical professional, no amount of telling her that she needs to get better is going to fix this. If you're applying pressure or maybe talking to her as though she is the one with the problem then you're barking up the wrong tree.

Recovery is a process, and one that requires time, patience and a lot of strength on the part of the sufferer. She can't wake up tomorrow and decides to turn over a new leaf and leave Bulimia behind. Her disorder is not a choice. This is something outside her control that is happening **to** her. As a caregiver and parent your job is assistance and support, **not** directing and pushing her to make progress before she is ready. Having a child with an eating disorder can leave many parents feeling powerless or unsure on how to help their daughter through this. You're the person that holds her hand through the tough times and is there to catch her when she falls, your advocate to health professionals, someone to make her laugh when she doesn't know she needs to and a consistent place of non-judgmental love, empathy and understanding. Imagine yourself feeling powerless, low about yourself and isolated and alone with your mental health, what would you want someone to tell you? What would you need?

THE BENEFITS OF FAMILY THERAPY

Bulimia is something that not only affects your daughter but affects the entire setting of your mealtimes as a family and should have brought change to many areas surrounding her disorder. Realistically this will be affecting your whole family, whether they are showing it or not. Having a sibling or child with an eating disorder is very hard and incredibly difficult to know how to navigate safely without causing further pain or discomfort to the sufferer. Family therapy offers a whole host of benefits not only for your teenager suffering with Bulimia but for the parents and siblings of the affected. Cognitive behavioral therapy or cbt has been found to be the most effective kind of therapy, above all others when treating both patients and their families for Bulimia. Family therapy coaches the entire family to work as one unit to help in developing healthier habits and thoughts around eating. (The American Journal of Physiotherapy, April 2018) It helps to give parents tools to be able to aid their child through the recovery process and also how they can be actively involved in the process. Not only is this greatly beneficial for the parents but also for the teenager who is suffering alone against Bulimia Nervosa.

If you've previously been the unhelpfully involved parent, this could be a great way of redirecting some of that need to be taking action into actually working with your daughter to help herself. For your daughter this could be an excellent opportunity to give her back the feelings of being 'normal' and to feel part of something again. The diagnosis of an eating disorder can be an isolating thing as you are immediately separated from your family and friends. It can feel like you're losing some of your identity with your diagnosis, despite it bringing about positive change. You look around and you're 'that girl' with eating problems. Her Bulimia diagnosis makes her feel like an outsider by default. Any setting where a group is present such as group or family therapy, helps to eliminate that feeling for your daughter and remind her that she is very much a part of something still and that her eating disorder is only a part of her. Through being present at therapy sessions it will also allow you to gain additional insight into your daughter's feelings. As we've discussed throughout this book, Bulimia and eating disorders as a whole are tightly woven into our emotions. So getting some insight on how your daughter truly feels, in her words will help you to gain that deeper level of understanding and in turn give her better support.

Google, forums and books like these are amazing educational tools and provide us with so much invaluable knowledge, but without talking individually to your daughter about her personal experiences with her Bulimia, you're going to lack the most valuable piece of the puzzle. Getting to grips on the emotional side of her disorder is the only way to be able to help your daughter. Hearing those hard to hear feelings or experiences that she is having will give you the tools you need to grasp this disorder for what it really is. Not only that but giving her the opportunity to have you there as an outlet and to provide assistance while talking things through at a therapy session. Attending therapy as a family offers you the chance to be an active part in the discussion and lets you be a fly on the wall to overhear her feelings, as well as being able to dive in with how that makes you feel with a supportive therapist present to provide guidance and clarification if needed.

The therapist will be able to provide some level of support not only to your teen but also to you too, as the tough conversations are happening rather than stewing on them for a week before you're given the assistance you need. Over-all, it provides an all-inclusive safe space for the entire family, drawing you all back together and making the recovery process a joint process. After all, it's undeniable that this has affected you all so why not work together to fight this disorder?

CONCLUSION

No matter the stage or age of your child, this **is** a terrifying thing for any parent and child to have to live through and you are absolutely justified in feeling that. An eating disorder of any kind doesn't come with a clear set of instructions or a manual, you're a parent but still a human being and are nearly guaranteed to get things wrong sometimes or be scared of what the future holds. It can be hard to wrap our logical minds around such an emotional issue, even more so with our parenting hat on. Emotional responses are a natural part of acceptance, so let yourself feel the tough stuff for a little while. Don't let that parental need to tackle this head control you and entice you into bottling up things that will later come out as problematic. Taking some positive action, whether that be agreeing to accompany your daughter to her first doctor's appointment, reinstating therapy that she once refused or just taking that first step to gain some wisdom on Bulimia, (such as choosing to read this book!) is an incredibly strong and commendable step for you as a parent and an ally to your daughter. While you're probably pressuring yourself into finding some kind of grandiose solution, there's little you can do as an external force. Bulimia isn't a problem to be fixed. Instead, refocus your attention towards the small pockets of opportunity that exist in your everyday life.

No matter how your teenager may seem like a reclusive and easily emotional stranger sometimes, they are still your daughter and are ultimately just a frightened child battling a very serious mental health condition. Your little girl is very much still there, she is just fighting against inconceivable demons. Now more than ever she needs your unconditional love and compassion, not to be a point of ridicule, mocking or dismissive behavior. You are human, but you are a human adult not a child, so don't let your emotions rule you and fall into emotionally immature and harmful habits. Love your daughter in the way that you'd want to be loved through this; gently and with all the advice and support you could get. Work as a team to help pull her back from the brinks of the darkness, don't leave her silently and invisibly flailing for help. Not only is this your daughter but this disorder has most likely caused tension and lots of upset to your family as a whole. Remember you guys are a family unit, you are a team. Neither you as a parent or your daughter as the sufferer is alone in this, you have each other. Therapy and medical advice are out there waiting to be called upon so whenever you and your daughter are feeling ready, get that in place and start reaping the rewards and benefits that that support can have.

Imagine your daughter's disorder like a wave. Full of highs and lows, ever changing and complex. All we can do is try to ride this wave of Bulimia as best as we can. We can't stop it or control it, so all we can do is learn to live alongside it more compassionately, ride the rough tides when they come and enjoy the more peaceful times when they arrive. Life is after all a unique experience for us all, this is just another stone to be paved of your daughter's journey through life. No doubt you had your struggles, trials and magical times throughout your lifetime too. This is just the varied beauty of life, it's different for us all. In the end, our experiences shape us into the strong individuals that we are meant to be, so that when the magical moments come, we can experience them at their fullest.

Bulimia can throw many parents off, and leave them feeling stuck on knowing what the next appropriate steps to take are so don't be disheartened if you're struggling to know how to handle this or feeling way out of your depth. You've reached the end of this book, so you should be armed with a varied arsenal of facts, information and ideologies to take away with you and feeling more confident in yourself now that you've taken some level of action to aid your daughter in her fight against Bulimia. You've done the right thing and even if you're still feeling uncertain of yourself, you should have some ideas to be able to have a think about or make a start on helping pave the way for your daughter's recovery.

BIBLIOGRAPHY

BEAT. (2022). *Home*. Beat. http://Beateatingdisorders.org.uk

Breathe Life Healing Centre. (2021). *Eating disorders*. http://breathelifehealingcentres.com

Child Welfare. (2019). *Home - Child Welfare Information Gateway*. Childwelfare.gov. http://childwelfare.gov

Community Eating Disorder Charity. (n.d.). *SupportED - The Community Eating Disorder Charity*. SupportED. Retrieved August 10, 2022, from http://supportedscotland.org

Ekern, B. (2019, April 9). *Eating disorders and control*. Eating Disorder Hope. http://EatingDisorderHope.com

Lauren Mulheim PsyPCEDS. (2021, April 29). *Eating disorders*. Verywell Mind. https://verywellmind.com

Le Grande PhD, D., Lock MDPhD, J., & Dymek PhD, M. (2018, April 30). *The American Journal Of Psyotherapy*. https://doi.org/10.1176/appi.phycotherapy.2003.57.2.237

MentalHelp.net. (2018). *Mental Health, Depression, Anxiety, Wellness, Family & Relationship Issues, Sexual Disorders & ADHD Medications*. Mentalhelp.net. http://mentalhelp.net

NHS Choices. (2020). *Bulimia Nervosa*. NHS. http://www.nhs.uk

NHS UK. (2019). *Bulimia Nervosa*. NHS. http://www.nhs.uk

Pietrangelo, A. (2019, March 15). *Healthline: Medical information and health advice you can trust*. Healthline.com. http://Healthline.com

Seeds Of Hope. (2020, December 23). *Eating Disorder Treatment for Adults and Adolescents*. Seeds of Hope. http://seedsofhope.pyramidhealthcarepa.com

Young Times. (n.d.). *Meal time idea's*. Retrieved August 10, 2022, from Youngtimes.org.uk